Alabama

MW00713133

Alabama's Favorite Folk Tales

Sarah Jane Turnbow Tackett

Seacoast Publishing, Inc.
Birmingham, Alabama

Sarah Jane Tackett

Published by Seacoast Publishing, Inc.
1149 Mountain Oaks Drive
Birmingham, Alabama 35226

ISBN 1-878561-56-1

To obtain copies of this book, please write
Seacoast Publishing, Inc.
Post Office Box 26492
Birmingham, AL 35226
or call
(205) 979-2909

Contents

The Tales

Dedication

To my precious family:
My husband, John Haynesworth,
and my daughters, Caroline and Rebecca

To my dear friends:
Bob and Sue Watters, who love storytelling as much as
I do.

Foreword

Long before the written tales ever existed, "living tales" were handed down from generation to generation in every corner of the world. These were the stories from Egypt, Africa, Rome, Israel—they were tales of war, of love, of adventure. Stories of great individuals were told, as well as stories about roaming bands of Gypsy folk. The tales traveled "on human tongue" from Turkey and Afghanistan to Spain and the British Isles. Eventually, they traveled to the Americas where they were joined by the tales of native people. Silver tongues wove the tales, while golden imaginations kept them alive. Folk tales were blown on the winds of the earth! Once a tale was spoken, it was free, to travel where ever the winds carried it, and be "recreated" as the next teller saw fit.

The first tales ever recorded in writing were put down on papyri in ancient Egypt. They were known as the *Tales of the Magicians.**

If memory preserves a tale, writing preserves it even better. Memories are often limited to the lifetime of specific generations, but the written word survives—and remains for others to enjoy.

Folk tales reflect our human condition. Like a treasure box, they are filled with the things we humans think, feel, say and do. Yet folk tales are like pools of water; they are not completely real, simply reflections. Still, we find ourselves in these reflections. We also find a part of our history in them.

My love for folk tales began with two people I loved as a child. The first was my father, Martin L. Turnbow. I spent many hours sitting in his lap when I was growing up. He told me wonderful stories that I could clearly see without the help of books or pictures. I especially remember going out to an open field, early one morning, with my father. He showed me silver cobwebs strewn across the field, glistening in the sunlight. He asked, "Sister, do you see all those tents? Some people call them spider webs, but their not! Why those are the tents of the fairy folk, and they're camped out all across this land."

"Can we see them?" I asked.

"Only if you approach them quiet as a little bird. Even then, they will most likely hear you coming and hide from you. It's enough that we can see their tents, and know that they are there."

To this very day I never see those sparkling webs that my heart doesn't skip a beat. It is imagination at its best, and a form of folk tale.

My grandmother Turnbow added to my love for tales. On rainy days, when I was small, she would pull the bedspread off the bed, drapping it around the front porch swing. Then she would line our six rocking chairs in rows of two, and tie the ropes to them. Here was our covered wagon with team of six to pull it. Next, grandmother would make up sandwiches, cookies and hot chocolate, then we would put pillows in the wagon, and off we would go on wonderful adventures "hardshipping through the mountains" together. Oh, the folk tales she would tell me then!

I once read that every story, no matter how absurd or far fetched, contains a certain amount of truth—even if that truth is as small as a grain of sand. Some of these tales are by now more fiction than fact, but fact or fiction, these are stories that have endured the test of time and are a part of the fabric that makes us, Alabamians, what we are.

After spending many years as an oral storyteller, and sharing with people age 3 to 93 in every conceivable situation, I can proudly say I have met many wonderful people throughout the state of Alabama.

It is my earnest hope that you will find some chuckles among the pages, as well as some discoveries. I found both as I collected them.

Here then are tales from and about Alabama. Read them, roll them across your tongue. Nothing warms the heart more than a good story.

*From *The Way of The Storyteller* by Ruth Sawyer.

Thanks

I want to thank my family for encouraging me to write. You have always given me a sense of accomplishment, companionship, and joy (as well as a wealth of story materials).

I want to thank Sue Watters, my "adopted sister," for listening more often than anyone else, and never saying 'I don't want to listen today.' Thanks for lending me your ear as I tried to put mental thoughts into readable words. Thanks too to Bob Watters for sharing so many tales with me.

I thank all the people who have shared their time and stories, allowing me to retell the tales in a storyteller's fashion.

Special thanks to Nell Turner Dirks for her valuable time proofreading, and editing my grammatical errors. What would I have done without you?

Thanks to all the libraries: Birmingham Public Library. Special thanks to Jim Pate, Southern History Department, for his many hours of patient assistance and help. Thanks to all within the Southern History and Archives Departments who were so willing to help me find facts I needed. Thanks to Homewood Library, North Shelby County Library, Samford University Library, Wheeler Regional Library, Lawrence County Library—special thanks to Virginia Johnson, Head Librarian, Jasper\Walker County Public Library, Dadeville Public Library.

Special thanks to Edward Herring for taking time to meet with me in Moulton to discuss his knowledge of Aunt Jenny Brooks.

Thanks to all the newspaper journalists and historians, past and present, who have helped preserve Alabama's wonderful history.

Thanks to Sandy Uptain for the loan of her very old Alabama history books for reference.

Thanks to all my loving friends who have listened, listened, listened, listened.

Thanks to my church family for all your prayers concerning my writing.

Thanks to the Birmingham Quill Club from whom I have learned so much about this art and who helped me meet my publisher.

Thanks to my publisher Janis Bailey and her husband Tom for giving me the opportunity to develop this book.

A House Divided

Talladega County, Alabama

Shortly after the turn of the 20th Century, two sisters were born in a small town in Talladega County. Their names were Sally Sadie and Sadie Sally. In reality, they were born the same year, the same month, the same week, the same day, the same hour, and almost the same minute!

Maternal twins, as much alike as two blades of grass, two drops of rain, or two kernels of corn. Each was small boned with fair almost transparent skin covered in freckles. Each had red hair and blue eyes. Not only did they look alike, they liked many of the same things. They liked red apples and the color yellow. They also liked cats and flowers. They minded their elders fairly well and were reasonably kind to strangers, but the likeness stopped right there.

Those girls had a flaw in their personalities. They couldn't get along at all—they quarreled all the time. I don't mean every now and then; I mean every solitary day. When they woke up one would say, "I can dress faster than you!" That would make the other one mad, and they would get into a fight. When they ate lunch one would say, "I don't slurp when I eat; you sound like a pig!" That would start another fight. Then at night when it was bedtime, one of them wanted to sleep with the light off, but the other one wanted to leave the light on so she could read. That caused a fight! The only time they didn't fight was when they were asleep. They looked like a couple of angels then.

Their quarreling was hard on everybody, particularly their poor mama! A kinder, sweeter woman you would never meet, but she cried a lot. (Why those two girls would make the gatekeeper of heaven cry.)

Their mama tried everything she could to make the twins get along. They had separate swings, separate toyboxes, and their beds were on opposite sides of the room. A red line marked the middle of the room. Each girl had her own space, but it didn't really help. One of them was forever yelling, "She's got her foot on my side of the room!" It was a mess.

Sally and Sadie quarreled when they were girls, and they quarreled when they were grown. They even quarreled after they married. Their husbands got along. Their children got along. Later, even their grandchildren and great-grandchildren got along, but not Sally and Sadie.

Time is a funny thing. It starts out slowly and picks up speed as it goes along. The years came and went. Before they knew it, Sally and Sadie were old. They couldn't hear well and they couldn't see clearly. Their arthritis and bursitis made them ache a lot. Both their husbands went on to eternal rest, and the children were busy most of the time, so the twins found themselves alone.

Maybe that's why they decided to buy back their father's house and move in together. No one was ever really sure why they did it, but they bought the house and remodeled it, painting it a weathered colonial yellow. Of course the quarrels began in no time. If Sadie made a soup, it wasn't salty enough for Sally.

If Sally let the cats in, Sadie put them back outside. Sadie liked the "easy chair" under the window but Sally liked it against the wall, and Sally liked the scatter rugs just tossed about, but Sadie wanted them in neat rows.

One day, the situation got to be too much, so they called a carpenter. They told him to saw the house down the middle from top to bottom! Then they had him put up a wall on the inside and seal the house back. When the carpenter finished, each sister had her own front door and back door. They put a fence in to divide the yards and a railing to divide the front porch.

Then a remarkable thing occurred. Sally and Sadie began to get along! For the very first time in their lives, they quit their quarreling. Everyone in town was astonished. They went shopping together and sat together in church. They visited over the back fence and invited one another over for dinner. It was the talk of the town, and it went on for years.

Sally and Sadie went out the same way they came in. They went out the same year, the same month, the same week, the same day and almost the same minute. Sally went out first, and Sadie cried so hard her blood pressure shot up. Sadie blew her top, so she went out next.

Their children had them buried side by side between their husbands. The twins shared a common gravestone, which read like this:

> Here lie Sally Sadie and Sadie Sally
> Like cats and dogs they fought..
> Till in their golden age their father's house they bought.
> They sawed it in half, to live apart,
> Somehow it changed their heart..
> Though quarreling was their fame, united they became.
> PEACE NOW AND EVERMORE!

A horsetrader told this tale and swore that every word is true. Of course names and exact location have been changed to prevent any quarrels.

Ruins of the old Virginia Mine in western Jefferson County

Willie Compton's Mining Tale

Jefferson County, Alabama

Unexplainable events happen almost daily in towns and cities all across the world. People, past and present, have left a trail of stories that tell about hearing voices or footsteps when no one is around, or objects that move on their own. Some tell of witnessing ghostly spectra's who make their appearances in haunted places.

If such things do occur on the earth's surface, what about the caverns and mines within the earth? Isn't it possible that the same eerie events have and do happen there as well?

Men and women who go down into deep mine shafts to work in tunnels and underground rooms are brave people. They don't all ways do the work by choice, but rather because of necessity. We human beings are not moles! Yet, like King Neptune's creatures who leave their salt-water world to scavenge food on land, miner's leave the earth's surface with it's green leaves and fresh air, to earn their wages beneath the ground.

There is a feeling when you descend into a mine. It is an unreal feeling, almost akin to diving in deep waters. A miner once said, "Every time you go down, you wonder if you'll ever be coming up again."

This thought is common among miners. Here in

Alabama generations of miners have gone down daily, and while most return safely, many have never come back.

Virginia Mines

People who live over in the area around the ruins of the Old Virginia Mines say that sometimes late in the evening, after it gets dark, you can hear weird sounds coming from the direction of the ruins. Some say they sound like low groaning noises, and others say you can hear sounds like hammers or axes falling. It is possible. There was a terrible disaster once in those mines.

Children used to work in the mines. Young children who should have been playing ball, or fishing. Boys used to go down and work in Alabama mines, just like they did in other places.

When the Virginia mines exploded in 1905, the earth shook. It was one of the worst mining explosions in Alabama history. At least that's what we've been told. The earth trembled that day, and red flames belched up from 500 feet underground! 112 miners lost their lives, including a young boy who was found with his daddy's coat over his head. It appeared like his daddy had covered him, trying to protect him from the coal dust, fire, and smoke.

Families waited above ground. Waited until it was clear enough for searchers to go down and look for bodies. There was much weeping that day.

Dynamite charges had to be set just right. If they were overcharged or undercharged, they would explode wrong. That's what happened down in the Virginia Mines. Methane was all around. Hissing like a snake! You can't see methane. You can't smell it, but you sure can hear it— hissing. There's no snake more dangerous than methane. When the dynamite exploded, all the gases exploded too. An explosion like that can make a fireball big enough to put the sun to shame. Those miners who died never stood a chance.

They closed Virginia Mines in 1953. Still, there are times when people hear strange, unexplainable noises around the whole area.

Willie Compton's Tale

The old man was withered with age. His dark, wrinkled flesh hung loosely over his once taunt muscles. Brown eyes that used to be bright, were now covered in the milky hue of age and cataracts. Still, his mind seemed sharp as he sat telling us about his days as a coal miner.

We asked, "What year were you born in Mr. Compton?"

"I was born in 1900. I'm 92 years old." He laughed. "I've lived a bit."

"How long did you work in the mines?"

He stared off into space, and then he said, "I went down in my first mine when I was eleven years old. Back then nobody cared if you was jest a little chile'. I had friends my age who worked underground too."

He paused as if collecting his thoughts. "Do you'all believe in supernatural things?" We shrugged our shoulders, "Maybe."

"When you work in the mines as long as I did, you get so you believe. I'm tellin' you, all kinds of things happen way down under the earth."

We asked, "Were you ever in a cave in?"

Willie Compton's eyes grew wide. "I almost was! It was a long time ago, but I couldn't ever forget it. It happened in 1957 while I was workin' in the Praco mines in West Jefferson county. I went down on a morn'in shift and I hadn't been workin' long when I started feelin' hungry. That was odd, cause' I ate me a big breakfast fore' I went to work that morn'in.

"Well, I just ignored my feelin's and kept right on workin' till I got so hungry it was almost like somthin' was nuddgin' me to go and eat. Then I felt someone staring at me and when I turned around I saw this fella standin' right there beside me. Scared me! He was dressed like a miner, but I never saw him before. He looked me straight in the eyes and he said, 'You need to go and eat, right now!' Then he just turned around and walked back out of my work area.

"I picked up my lunch pail and walked out right after him, but he was gone when I came out. I hadn't walked very far when the place where I was workin' caved in! No one ever knew what happened. It might have been a rock fall, or it might have been a methane explosion. I never heard a boom sound, like an explosion makes, but ever what it was knocked me off my feet. Coal dust was so thick ya couldn't hardly breath. Two men were killed that morn'in. It happened at nine o'clock and I walked out of there just a few minutes before nine. If I had stayed I most likely would have been killed too.

"I've tried to tell folks about that stranger sometimes, but nobody be'leves me. I spec' nobody be'leves somethin' less it happens to them. It don't matter. Once ya see some'thin strange like I did—you know its real whether no one else be'leve it or not! I do wonder sometimes though, why you spose' that fella', or whoever he was, come to save me that morn'in?

No one can ever be certain about such phenomena as Willie Compton experienced. Perhaps we never will—in this life. Too many people have witnessed such things, and too many tales have been told about them, to just discard the information as nonsense.

Sources: Articles from newspaper accounts and oral tradition.

"Once ya see some'thin strange like I did—you know its real whether no one else be'leve it or not."
—Willie Compton

Midnight Ashes

Wilcox County, Alabama

Eszra Tylor turned over in bed, his eyes open. He could hear his mule braying. Eszra stared out the open window. October's moonlight bathed the trees in a pale glow. He sat up in the bed when he heard his mule galloping away. Eszra knew Casaundra was gone again. It was the third time this week. What was he to do?

He lay his head back on the pillow, recalling how he'd met Casaundra Verneuille. She was working as a cook for ol' Miz Lambert. He had gone there to carry Miz Lambert's new pie-safe to her. When he tapped on the back door, Casaundra opened it. She was the most beautiful woman he had ever seen. Her aqualine facial features betrayed French or Indian blood. Her skin was smooth, the color of mellowed maple. Her hair and eyes were black. It was her eyes that captivated him. Their expression was so deep he was unable to do anything but stare at her.

"What you want?" she asked.

"I built a new safe for Miz Lambert's pies and such," he said. "It's out in my wagon. I need to bring it in and put it over yonder in the corner. 'Fore I put the new one in here, I got to take the doors off the ol' one and empty it so's I can pull it outside."

She stepped back to let him in, then watched him

without a word. After removing the doors, he tilted the old pie-safe and began to move it out. She opened the back door for him. In a few minutes he brought the new safe indoors, resting it on an old quilt. He set the safe up in the corner. She watched as he put four doors on it, two long doors on the top, two small doors on the bottom. The top doors contained hammered tin work cut in diamond designs.

"You do good work." She said it as though they had been talking with each other. "You're good with your hands. I think you're lucky you was trained as a carpenter before freedom come, Eszra Tylor."

The look in her dark eyes made him feel like it was hard to breath. "How you know my name?"

She smiled.

He fumbled for words, then said, "You new here?"

"You know I am, Eszra Tylor! You never seen me before, has you?"

Again he asked, "How you know my name?"

"I know lots of things," she said. "I know your mule's 'bout to throw a shoe on its front right foot. You be wise to stop by the blacksmith shop 'fore you go much further today. I also know your cow is sick in your barn. Snake bit her yesterday in your pasture. You kill one of your black chickens when you go home today. Split that chicken in half, make a poultice for your cow's leg. Keep the poultice on till all the chicken meat turns green. That'll draw the poison out of the bite, then your cow will recover."

Eszra looked dumbfounded. "How you know these things?"

She laughed. "I just know, Eszra!"

After that day he saw Casaundra in many different places. He saw her at the creek and at the market square. He even saw her at the corn mill. She always smiled at him. He learned her name, and that she had come from Mobile. Thomas Haygood said to him, "She's a Creole woman, Eszra, stay away from her. She's into all kinds of strange ways. Some folks say she may be a witch. Stay away from her, my friend."

One morning when Eszra opened his cabin door, Casaundra was standing there. "I've come to talk with you, Eszra Tylor." Her smile made his heart skip a beat. "Will you invite me in?" He moved aside as she stepped into his cabin. Her presence made him feel uneasy. He felt self-conscious so he left the cabin door ajar. She seemed to read his thoughts. "I won't bite you, Eszra."

They sat down at his table and Casaundra talked. "I've need of a husband," she said. "People are talking about me. People like your friend Thomas Haygood. I think mostly they can't accept a woman who's a stranger in their midst. Specially a Creole woman without a husband. I've decided to marry you, Eszra; you'll make me a fine husband."

He must have looked startled because she began to laugh. "Don't be so shocked," she said. "I'll make you a good wife too. You'll be a happy man, I promise you that."

Once he recovered he said, "Even if I was able to take me a wife, which I ain't, what makes you think I'd want to marry you?"

"Cause' you think I'm beautiful. Your mouth goes dry anytime you're around me. Oh, you'll wed me all right, Eszra Tylor, 'fore the next full moon."

They talked awhile and Casaundra shared a little of her past with him. She began by saying, "I come from the bayou country down below Mobile. A place called Coq'd Inde. Jean Baptiste Le Moyne, Sieur de Bienville named it. It means 'turkey gobbler.'" She laughed and then she asked, "Did you know my father was an alligator?"

"What?" He thought he had heard her wrong.

"Yes," She laughed. "Haven't you ever heard of such a thing?"

"Never!"

"Well, the bayou's be full of such tales. My mama was just fourteen years old. She was standin' by the water's edge washin' some clothes when this big ol' gater come crashin' up out of there, and catched her with his great, long, white teeth! He starts draggin' her into the water, her just beggin' for her life. Mama was real pretty an that gater he taken with her. He thinkin', what a waste to kill her. So he didn't."

"You tellin' me a gator was your pa?"

She smiled and nodded her head.

"You believe that?" he asked.

Her expression changed. "I used to believe it when I was little. I'd go down to the edge of the bayou and holler for my pa! I hated him then cause he never come round me and mama. Times so hard, we almost starve to death." She paused. "Mama work herself into a early grave. I just ten years old when she die. That's when the ol' women took me in to live with 'em."

"What ol' women?"

She smiled, her beautiful eyes sparkling. "The ol' women what teached me all I know, Eszra."

He wanted to ask her more about it, but wasn't so sure he really wanted to know.

Casaundra got up from her chair and walked over to the open door. Standing in the doorway she said, "I's 18 years old when I met a man from Mobile. I followed him there."

Eszra was drawing on the table with his finger and didn't look up, but he listened.

"His name was Marcus, he was a good man—a Creole man. He was good to me."

She paused again, staring out the doorway. Then she shrugged her shoulders and said, "Marcus die of Yellow Jack." She didn't elaborate. "I work for Miz Lambert's sister and her husband after he die. They the ones who bring me here." Her voice took on a longing sound, "Sometimes, Eszra, I miss the smells of the bayou and those ol' bull gators roaring at night. Some day I want to go back."

Then she laughed again, and her laughter sounded like music.

"Now tell me 'bout you." She sat back down at the table.

He began with a question. "You was never a slave?"

She shook her head. "Mama was a slave. She belonged to a Frenchman. He 'cided to go back to France and freed mama 'fore he went. I was born later."

"You lucky." He said it with a frown on his face. Then he shared with her what life had been like as a slave, back before freedom came. "I guess I was lucky in a way too. My daddy was taught carpentry and I learned it from him." When he finished, she touched his hand. It felt as if someone had touched him with a fire brand.

Casaundra was right. They wed in September 1885. For a while it was a good marriage. Eszra was happy. Casaundra kept the cabin clean, prettying it up with curtains. She added some new furniture. Her cooking was excellent and her laughter contagious. He found himself laughing more and more.

Casaundra hadn't lived in the cabin long however, when strange things started to occur. Cats appeared, refusing to leave. Black cats. Then a crow took up residence in a big oak next to the cabin. It cawed day and night, almost driving Eszra mad. He shot at it with his gun, but the crow just flew off, returning when Ezra went inside.

Frogs were everywhere. At night the outdoors sounded as if they were living in a deep swamp. Hundreds of bats circled the cabin in the evenings. It was scary. Casaundra seemed untroubled. "They're just harmless animals," she said.

By August the following year, Casaundra started leaving the house around midnight on nights when the moon was full. When he questioned her about it she answered, "I was in the bed beside you, Eszra; you must be dreaming." She would never admit to anything. When he waked and found her gone, he was too sleepy to get out of bed to look for her. She was always beside him in the mornings. Eszra thought maybe she was right. Maybe he was having a recurring dream.

Then she began to ride his mule. The poor animal was so tired in the daytime it could barely work for him. When he told her to stop, she looked irritated. "Eszra, if your mule is tired, perhaps it's because the animal is growing old. You expect too much from the beast. Why in the world would I want to ride your mule?"

When Eszra shared his concerns with Thomas Haygood, Thomas said, "I warned you, Eszra. I told you some folks called her a witch. Mae Foster says witches love to ride across the fields when the moon is full. May says they take off their clothes and shed their skins, then they ride in their skeleton bones. You got you a bad problem, Eszra."

When he came home after talking with Thomas, Eszra asked Casaundra point blank, "Is you mixed up in hoodoo?"

She laughed at him. "Don't be a fool, Eszra. When you gonna stop listen'n to such crazy talk?"

Ezra didn't mean to, but he picked at her more and more. They quarreled a lot.

Eszra pushed the bedcovers back and sat up. He was so sleepy he could hardly stand, but he made himself get out of bed. "She must be puttin' somethin' in my food on nights she leaves," he muttered. He managed to pull on his pants and shirt, then lit the lamp and walked down to the barn.

When he reached the mule's stall, Eszra found it empty. It wasn't a dream. Looking around, he noticed something lying in a pile on the floor of the stall. It was Casaundra's clothing. Something else lay beside the clothes. Bending down, he saw it was some kind of mellow, maple-colored leather. He touched it and flinched.

All the various warnings he had heard from Thomas Haygood poured into Eszra's mind. Was it possible? If Thomas was right, it would explain all the strange things Casaundra did. How she knew so much about people and seemed to read their thoughts. It also explained the sudden appearance of the cats and the crow, the frogs and bats. He'd never seen such things around his place before Casaundra came to live there.

Eszra slowly picked up the clothing and leather. He

walked out of the barn, gathering up sticks and leaves. He started a fire. When it was hot, he tossed Casaundra's things into the flames. After the fire burned itself out, Eszra raked up all the ashes. He put them into an old crockery jar and sealed the lid. Then he walked over to his well and dropped the jar in. He heard a splash when the jar hit the bottom of the well.

Eszra's mule never returned, and he never saw Casaundra again. Oddly, no one ever asked about her. It was as though she had never existed. When he mentioned what had happened to Thomas Haygood, Thomas looked at him with a puzzled expression and said, "It's just as well, Eszra. She was strange. It's good you dropped those things into your well. I'm sure she will never come back here."

All the animals disappeared the night Casaundra left. Eszra Tylor changed after that. He lost interest in everything, becoming a withdrawn, solemn man. Eventually he moved away from Wilcox County. No one was ever sure where he went. Some folks said he moved somewhere down on a bayou near Mobile.

This is an old tale. It has been told in one way or another for generations in Wilcox County. There are variants found in many countries of the world.

Ragland children ready to hand-cut fodder from corn field

Mysterious Tales From Bibb County

Bibb County, Alabama

The Old Graveyard

If you drive down highway 82, from Tuscaloosa to Prattville, in some areas you cross low hills, dense woods and farmland. There are many small towns along the route. They include: Duncanville, Hagler, Eoline, Centerville and Lawly.

Eoline is small. Very small. Some people have nick-named Eoline, "end-of-the-line." Yet it, like so many little towns in Alabama, has a long history dating back to the early 1800s.

About a mile and a half from Eoline, off County Road 16 which goes to Pondville, there's an old cemetery sitting up in the woods by itself. Many gravesites can no longer be distinguished since trees and undergrowth cover them. Plain wooden crosses that used to mark the graves have long since rotted. Some of the gravesites are marked with large rocks dug from the surrounding area. Names and dates have been chiseled into them. There are a few granite markers too, but not many. This old graveyard was abandoned more than 50 years ago.

Back in 1950, John and Rosa Mae Ragland owned the

land that encompassed the old cemetery. John's brother, Harvey G. Ragland, had a home about a quarter mile from it. All the Ragland land was deeded to their great grandfather through a land grant before the Civil War.

Harvey G. and Vashti Ragland raised a family of eight children on their farm. In 1950, seven children remained at home. They included three boys and four girls.

Cemeteries have all ways held a special fascination for young children, especially those who live near them. Maybe such places help them connect with the past and ponder mortality. It was natural for the Ragland children to spend many hours playing in the old graveyard on their uncle John's land. They would walk among the headstones and wonder who lay buried beneath them.

The children developed games connected to the markers. One game involved finding the oldest dated stone or a particular name, then taking turns telling stories about the occupant. Sometimes the stories were scary, building momentum with each telling until they became too real—then all the children would run for home!

One day something happened in the old cemetery that changed the children's attitude toward the place. It happened one September afternoon when all the children had some time to play before dinner. They headed for the cemetery. The leaves on the big oaks surrounding the graves were beginning to change colors. Acorns littered the ground, and made crunching sounds as the siblings walked on them.

They noticed something different immediately. Pausing, they saw that two of the graves, which lay side by side, had sunk about four or five feet. These graves contained two brothers. Their rock gravestones read:

William Underwood
Born: November 15, 1802
Died: October 10, 1826

Philip Underwood
Born: July 23, 1804
Died: October 10, 1826

These were two of the children's favorites. They loved

making up stories about how the Underwood brothers died. As they stood there gazing into the holes, the Ragland children knew that new graves sometimes dropped when they settled, but these graves were over 100 years old. This made them wonder if someone had been digging in the old cemetery.

One of them said, "We ought to fill these holes back up, it's the least we can do for them." They all agreed, and set about gathering rocks, limbs, pinecones, straw, and dirt to refill the holes. The job took about two hours to finish. Once it was finished, the graves were ground level again. The children scattered a layer of newly fallen leaves over the top of each one.

That night, after supper was finished, the children headed outside for a game of *kick the can*. As darkness crept in, they settled on the front porch to rest and talk. They hadn't been there very long when Maude, the oldest girl, pointed across the peanut field in the direction of the woods. The children watched, as in the dim moonlight, two men walked out of the woods and started across the freshly plowed field toward the Ragland house. All the brothers and sisters knew that nothing lay beyond the woods except the graveyard, and a large swamp on the other side of it.

As the men drew closer, the children sat frozen in their seats. There appeared to be an eerie glow encircling each man. They were dressed in dark pants, and wore white shirts, and wore hats on their heads. When the men got about 30 yards from the house, they stopped. Slowly, each man lifted his hat from his head and tipped it, nodding. Then they made an abrupt turn, and headed off down the lane toward the road.

As soon as the men were gone, the children ran into the house, relating the entire story to their father. He listened intently, and when they had finished he said, "Tomorrow morning we'll go look at the graves."

The Ragland children were up and dressed before the rooster crowed the next morning. As they walked across the peanut field with their father, they noticed that the only footprints in the soft soil were the ones they had left the day before. None of the footprints resembled man-size shoes. When they pointed this out, Mr. Ragland remained silent.

He was in the lead when they arrived at the cemetery and said, "I thought you kids told me you filled these graves yesterday." The children were startled when they looked at the graves. The holes had returned. Only now, stacked neatly at the foot of each grave, were the rocks, limbs, pinecones, straw, and dirt they had used to fill the holes. Mr. Ragland studied the graves a few minutes, then he said, "Let's go home."

When they reached the house, he had the children sit down around the kitchen table. Looking into their faces, he said, "I don't claim to understand any of this. I don't think it's necessary for us to understand it, and there's no need to be afraid either. When I was a boy, I used to play in that old graveyard same as you kids do now. I once found a sunken grave, just as you did. I was standing there looking at it when I caught a glimpse of something out of the corner of my eye. When I turned and looked toward the swamp woods, nothing was there. It scared me, so I lit out for home. Never went back there much after that."

Eventually, the Ragland children played in the old graveyard again. William and Paul Underwood's graves remained untouched.

Ruination Swamp

Ruination Swamp is a name some locals call the a swamp that meanders through a 10 to 12 mile section of Bibb County. It is created by the overflow of Ingate and Mooney creeks before they reach the Cahaba River.

The swamp contains many small animals and reptiles such as water moccasin, deer, fox, turkey, bobcats, raccoon, possum, squirrels, and a few black bear. Insects and hundreds of croaking frogs call this swamp home too.

Over the last 100 years, several people have been lost in this swamp. It's easy to happen since everything looks so much alike once your in it. Moss grows on all sides of the trees.

Back around 1896, Hubert Mooney got himself lost in the swamp. Only Hubert never came out again. No one really knows for sure what happened to Hubert. He knew that swamp like the back of his hand. He grew up living along side of it, and he played in it as a boy. Hubert spent a lot of time hunting in the swamp as a man too.

Then one day Hubert Mooney just walked off without saying a word to anyone. He left his two hunting hounds at home. His sister watched him go into the swamp, but nobody ever saw him come out again. His brothers said, "Quicksand must 'ave got him. We looked, but we never found no trace of him. A 'moccasin may have bit him!" It was after Hubert's disappearance that some called the swamp, Ruination.

Fifty-six years later, on a lazy Sunday afternoon in the summertime, young Sewilla Ragland and her seven brothers and sisters became lost in Ruination swamp. It was 1952.

Sunday, at the Ragland house, was the Lord's Day.

They followed their Missionary Baptist tradition of church, dinner and rest. The problem was, the Ragland children seldom, if ever, rested unless they were asleep. Sunday was their day to play.

Some Sundays the children would play in the "gully." This was a large sand wash-out near their home. The siblings took turns climbing the steep sides of the gully, then sliding back down again. Sometimes they dug caves into its sides, large enough to crawl inside. Both of these games were dangerous since the gully was prone to cave-ins.

Other Sundays the children would cut grass and dirt blocks out of the pasture. This they would use to build a dam to stop the flow of water bubbling out of the family's fresh water spring. It created an excellent swimming hole four to five feet deep.

On this particular Sunday afternoon, however, they decided to play on the "Island." This was a piece of land that lay three or four miles from their house—deep inside Ruination swamp. The land was surrounded by shallow water, mud and muck.

Before they left, the children asked their mother if they could have their daddy's plow lines. She agreed, cautioning them to return the lines when they finished so their daddy would have them on Monday morning.

The children went to the barn and collected the plow lines, then headed for the "Island."

When the adventurers arrived, the first thing they did was tie the plow lines between the trees. Then they began throwing branches over the lines, creating an imaginary Indian encampment. It took them a long time to get it just right, but when they did, they played for several hours.

Darkness can fall on a swamp unnoticed, like a feather falling from the sky. It began to grow dark. Landcey, the oldest boy, said, "We've really goofed. We better get out of here before it gets so dark we can't see!"

They pulled down the plow lines and started out of the swamp. Landcey was right. Darkness enveloped them.

Landcey was a good woodsman and navigator; he guided his brothers and sisters in the direction he thought would take them out of the swamp. In a few minutes, Sewilla sobbed, "We're lost Lancey!" By then, it was so dark the children could barely see their hands if they were close to their faces.

Landcey was smart. He took the plow lines and said, "Here, all of you catch hold of these lines. Don't you turn loose of 'em."

The brothers and sisters did just what he told them to do. Sewilla moved up next to Landcey, and Maude, the oldest girl, followed at the rear. As they walked along, Sewilla quit crying because she had absolute faith in her big brother. She had no idea how lost Landcey really was.

They must have walked through that swamp for a half mile or more, bogging in the mud, and listening to it's many sounds. Suddenly Landcey stopped. "Look!," he whispered. In front of them, maybe a hundred yards or so, they saw a light. It hung suspended like someone standing there with a lantern in their hand.

"There's daddy!" Sewilla squealed.

The light swayed side to side for a few seconds, then moved off through the darkness. Landcey led the children as he followed the lantern. It took them in a straight line, out of the swamp to the back fence that surrounded the corn field. The corn rows ran in the direction of the Ragland's back porch. When they reached the fence, the light disappeared.

Sewilla said, "Daddy's gone on home."

The children were so relieved to be safely out of the swamp, they jumped up and down, and hugged each other. Later, as they walked through the kitchen door, they saw Harvey G. and Vashti Ragland seated at the kitchen table with worried expressions on their faces. Mr. Ragland looked relieved as he said, "It's about time you kids got home. I was going to give you five more minutes, then I was coming to look for you!"

Many people have different theories about what happened that summer night in Ruination swamp. Some say it was swamp gas the children saw. Other's think it was the haint of ol' Hubert Mooney that led the children to the corn field. Vashti Ragland, however, was a praying mother. She always said, "The Lord is good. He sent one of his angels to led my children to safety!"

These stories have long been told as oral tales by Sewilla (Sue) Ragland Watters, a well-known Alabama oral storyteller.

Then one day Hubert Mooney just walked off without saying a word to anyone. He left his two hunting hounds at home. His sister watched him go into the swamp, but nobody ever saw him come out again. His brothers said, "Quicksand must 'ave got him. We looked, but we never found no trace of him. A 'moccasin may have bit him!" It was after Hubert's disappearance that some called the swamp Ruination.

Aunt Jenny's Tales of Woe

Lawrence County, Alabama

An old woman once lived under the shadows of the government woods in Lawrence County. Some folks liked her and some feared her. Regardless, they all had tales to tell about her—tales that are still told today.

There are those who still call Aunt Jenny a witch. They say she did strange things—washing her hands in a human skull shaped like a large half gourd. Others tell of times she was seen walking or riding through the deep woods late at night, talking and laughing as if she was enjoying someone's company. Yet she was alone. They say Aunt Jenny didn't like people, preferring her own fellowship.

Folks who liked her tell a different tale. They were quick to say, "She surely wasn't a witch. Why the tales of the human skull came from her own lips. She was fond of storytelling. She loved nothing better than to spin such yarns to a group of children, and then watch their eyes grow wide."

"As far as her being in the woods at night," they continued, "she was a healer and a midwife. She used ancient arts, passed down from her Cherokee ancestry. Aunt Jenny knew all the herbs. She knew their healing powers. She would give the sick bitter-sweet to calm them, and bloodroot for whooping cough. She knew the root bark of burning bush would help the dropsy. Sure Aunt Jenny rode and walked all hours of the day and night. She delivered hundreds of babies, taking care of their mothers until they were strong again. Aunt Jenny never charged a penny for her help. She was admired and respected. As for her preferring to be alone, that's not true either. Her latch was open to anyone who cared to sit and talk a spell."

Aunt Jenny Brooks Johnston lead a dual life. The past was hard, much harder than most people in our modern day can imagine. Alabama was still a wilderness. Circumstances surrounded Jenny that she could not control. Regardless of the stories, she was a woman of legendary fame. A story-teller for sure, but not all her tales were created. She was often heard to say, "Come listen to my tales of woe."

She was born Louisa Elizsabeth Jane Bates January 22, 1826 in Kentucky,. Her parents, James and Annie Bates, were a part of the human sea that rolled westward. They arrived in Alabama sometime between 1826 and 1833. They later migrated to Texas, but by that time Jenny had met and married Willis Brooks. She was a beautiful black-haired, blue-eyed half-Cherokee girl of fifteen. Willis was thirty-five. They married in Tuscaloosa Ccounty, June 17, 1841.

They lived in several places, but eight years later Willis bought forty acres near Mount Hope in what was once called the Black Warrior Forest. Their farm sat at the fork of Byler and Kinlock roads. The old Byler Road was an important stagecoach road connecting Tuscaloosa and Nashville, Tennessee. It had originally been part of an Indian trail called the High Town Path. Willis slowly increased his land holdings over the years, and he and Jenny opened their cabin as a roadhouse for travelers. When Aunt Jenny died, at the age of 98, she had lived on the same farm more than eighty years.

Willis and Jenny had ten children. Nine lived and one died in infancy. For any woman to lose a single child is more pain than the heart can bear, yet Aunt Jenny later lost five sons and eventually buried all but one of her children, as well as two husbands. It was a bitter cup.

Tales of Woe

Aunt Jenny's first tale of woe began during the Civil War. Feuds had been common in the mountains, but once the war started neighbors were divided. Some opposed secession, while the Confederate home guards were determined that every able-bodied man would serve the Confederate cause. Ill feelings erupted into deadly gun fights.

Some people claim that Willis served as a Confederate soldier while others say he never did. Regardless, a neighbor began to trouble Jenny and her daughters. Willis shot and killed the offender. Soon afterward, a band of home guards rode onto the Brooks farm and a gunfight broke out. Both Willis and his oldest son, John, were killed.

Aunt Jenny took up Willis's gun, shooting one of the intruders on the spot. She always referred to the man as a "Yankee," but the term *Yankee* was used loosely at the time. Jenny gathered all her children around her and vowed to avenge their father's death. Eight men were implicated in the murders. An article, written in the February 2, 1920 edition of *The Birmingham News* quotes Aunt Jenny as saying, "Seven of 'ems been got."

Within weeks of Willis's and John's deaths, trespassers again rode onto the Brooks farm. This time they burned Jenny's house and out buildings. She was a thirty-eight-year-old widow woman with eight children.

The war continued, but somehow Jenny managed to rebuild. Seven years later she married Jacob Strauter Johnston. Jacob moved onto her farm with his children, and Jenny raised this family as well as her own.

During these years Aunt Jenny was active as a midwife and healer throughout the Bankhead area. Still, her woes continued. She lost four sons, some of her grandsons, and one son-in-law in gun fights. The gun battles reached as far as Indian Territory. One son, Mack, disappeared while helping drive cattle along the Chisholm Trail. After Mack disappeared, one of her daughters died of measles.

Henry Brooks was Aunt Jenny's last remaining son. He lost his right leg in a Texas gunfight, and lived in Oklahoma Indian Territory five years. He returned to Alabama in 1911 to care for his mother. Henry married one year later, settling down with a family of his own. He did odd jobs and was generally liked by his neighbors. They spoke of him doing kind acts for them. In spite of this new life, Henry's past was filled with feuds and gun battles, and because of this he had many enemies.

Henry Brooks operated a whiskey still, never considering it wrong. He followed an old recipe his ancestors had used for centuries. However, the government was growing, and the government was against moonshiners. On January 11, 1920 a posse of officers from Winston County surrounded Henry at his still. He had a loyal, trustworthy horse he had named *Henry* after himself. The horse was trained to make sounds if anyone approached, which he did. Henry was prepared to fight when the posse arrived. It was twenty to one that day. Both Henry and his beautiful horse ended up dead. Jenny would later say, "All my sons was good men; they all died with their boots on."

One of the babies Aunt Jenny delivered during her years as a midwife grew up to become a Missionary Baptist preacher. She enjoyed listening to him preach in her later years, and was very fond of him. It was the Reverend Buttrum who influenced Jenny's decision to join the church. On the day she was baptized, church members carried her into the baptismal waters seated in a chair.

When Aunt Jenny Brooks Johnston died on March 29, 1924, it was a sad day for many people in the Mount Hope and Moulton area. They knew, loved and treasured this old mountain woman. This woman with the laughing blue eyes, free-flowing creative tongue, and sage advisor to all who would learn from her long road in life.

Sources: Wheeler Regional Library; Lawrence County Public Library; newspaper articles; papers written by Thomas C. Pettus and Edward Herring. One interview with Mr. Edward Herring proved very helpful. His wife, Helen, was Aunt Jenny's great-great-great granddaughter. Special thanks to Virginia Johnson, Head Librarian, Lawrence County Public Library and librarians at Wheeler Regional Library.

The Backwoods Preachers "Sons of Thunder"

Butler County, Alabama

Religious instruction first came to Alabama through the efforts of Catholic priests, both Spanish and French. A church was established in Mobile in 1704. The Anglican church first made an appearance in Mobile in 1763. In 1827, the Reverend Robert Davis established a church in Tuscaloosa, and by 1831 there were parishes in Greensboro and Huntsville.

The Baptist founded the Flint River congregation in 1808, led by Reverend John Nicholson. The Flint River church had a membership of 12 people at that time. Within a year, Enon Church was formed in Huntsville. This later became the First Baptist Church of Huntsville.

A church was organized by the Presbyterians in Huntsville in 1818. Bethel Church was formed in Tuscaloosa in 1820. Cahaba was the site of the Presbytery of Alabama, and was organized in 1821.

The Reverend Matthew P. Sturdivant came into the territory from South Carolina in 1808 as an official missionary of the Methodist Society. Reverend Michael Burge, of Georgia later joined Reverend Sturdivant. The organi-

zational meeting of the first Alabama Methodist Conference was in 1832, reporting a membership of 12,000 Methodists.

These denominations were the first to gain a foothold in Alabama. Others soon followed. The first Jewish synagogue was built in Mobile in 1844. Until then, Jewish worshipers celebrated the Sabbath in private homes.

The Backwoods Preachers

Sometime around 1803 Lorenzo Dow, a self-styled Methodist circuit rider, put his wife on his horse behind him and began to travel into the Tombigbee area preaching to settlers and Indians alike. A few years later, Alexander Travis, a Baptist circuit preacher and nephew of William Barrett Travis who fought at the Alamo, walked 25 to 35 miles each day preaching among the Indians. Travis continued his circuit from 1810-1852.

Circuit riders and evangelists brought many churches into being. They traveled the backwoods and trails, 'blowing the trumpet' and preaching God's word wherever they could find enough seating to hold a crowd. Sometimes they met in school houses, sometimes they held their meetings in saloons, and sometimes meetings were held out in the open. It depended upon space, weather and number of people. Later, as camp meetings became popular, communities established camp areas for visiting preachers. Neighbors and friends would gather to sing and listen to all-day preaching.

In the early frontier days, settlements were spaced about. Preaching was seldom heard, and much of the population was given to rough behavior. Needy prodigals spent their time fighting, and drunkenness was common. Mothers and wives often longed for the circuit riders to hold their meetings, in the hope that family situations might be improved.

It must be said that there were criminal types who took advantage of the welcome that circuit riders received from

Alabama's isolated settlements. Thieves often pretended to be ministers, then stole from those who attended their meetings. Even so, many fine preachers, who were sincere in their efforts, rode the circuits. These good ministers were a breed unto themselves. They were often determined, fearless men, the converts of other circuit riders and evangelists, not long removed from their own types of "rough behavior." They knew that of which they preached, and had great zeal to see souls won over from 'the gaul of bitterness and the bonds of iniquity.' Not all converts maintained changed lives, as many church records prove, but many were changed for the good and remained so throughout their lifetime.

Sons of Thunder

It was in late spring of 1832 when Buck Miller walked out of his cabin slamming the door behind him. He could hear his wife, Mary Elms, weeping as he left. Buck climbed on his horse and kicked it hard. The animal jumped forward breaking into a full gallop. Buck turned the horse toward Pigeon Creek. He could hear Mary Elms calling to him as he rode away, "Buck!"

As long as Buck had known her, Mary Elms had been a devoted reader of the Good Book. Come Sunday of any week she refused to do work that wasn't absolutely necessary for the care and feeding of her family. "Sunday is the Lord's Day," she would say. She insisted that her children hold a form of church within their home on the Lord's Day, complete with singing, Bible reading and teaching. Buck was tolerate of her, considering he knew how she was before he ever married her. Just so long as she didn't expect anything from him. It was a mutual agreement they had lived with for many years.

Then that "Travelin' Preacher" Beecher Anderson came around and messed up everything. Everybody in the settlement, and for miles around, went to hear him preach.

Mary Elms insisted upon going. Buck had no interest in seeing him. No sir. He had about as much interest in that preacher as he did in a rattlesnake.

Well, Mary Elms kept on about it, until Buck finally hitched the mule to the wagon and carried her and the children to Georgiana, the nearest settlement to their farm. The local mercantile served as the meetin' place.

After Buck dropped his family off, he went to the blacksmith shop to visit with his friend Will Cranshaw. Will was repairing a wagon wheel, and Buck offered his help. He knew a lot about smithing, and often helped Will. When they finished, they sat outside the blacksmith shop talking. "It's rare for us to have a preacher," said Will. Buck didn't reply.

"My wife wants me to go with her to hear him when he comes back this way. I suppose I'll go just to please her."

Buck still didn't reply.

"You know Buck this is only the second travelin' preacher I can remember ever comin' here."

Two too many, Buck was thinking. *This ain't gonna do nothin' but stir Mary Elms up; we'll have trouble because of it.*

He was right. Mary Elms was a fine woman. Loyal and hard working—but she spent too much time thinking about God. Religion was a source of contention between them, and it always led to him needing to change his ways. Life was hard enough in the backwoods, and be darned if he was going to give up the few things that gave him pleasure. *A little whiskey and gambling never hurt nobody.* He finally told her he didn't want to hear about it anymore. She quit pushing him after that, but she was adamant about Sundays and about teaching their children right ways.

The morning after the preaching, Mary Elms started in on him. They quarreled until it escalated to the point she was crying. Finally she said, "I've had enough of your wild ways Buck Miller! I'm a good wife to you. I'm thinking now that maybe I would like to return to Charleston to my family."

When she said that, Buck went crazy. "It's that puff-cheeked preacher's fault," he shouted. "I'll kill him for causing this."

"No Buck!" Mary Elms cried. "It ain't the preacher what's caused our trouble. It's been comin' a long time now. Maybe I should've never married you."

Buck walked out then, slamming the door behind him. He knew the travelin' preacher was on his way down Pigeon Creek, heading for the next settlement. Buck turned his horse south, cutting through the woods. He knew more about the countryside that that pompous church strutter, and would be waiting when Beecher Anderson rode past on his way down the creek.

The wait didn't take long. Buck was hiding behind a thick stand of trees when he heard Preacher Anderson coming. The man was singing in a loud, booming voice, "Oh how happy are they who the Savior obey..."

Buck's face turned livid! He kicked his horse and, riding out, he blocked the preacher's path. When preacher Anderson saw Buck he smiled and said, "Good day to you brother."

"Don't you call me your brother you piece of pious cloth! I've come out here to teach you a few things about the backwoods." Buck jumped down from his horse. "Climb off that horse!" he shouted.

The preacher continued to smile at him. "What's your name brother?" He asked his question as though Buck had never spoken a word to him.

"Didn't you hear me? I told you to climb down off of that horse. I'm here to beat you senseless!"

The preacher looked down at him with an almost quizzical expression. "Hold on now brother! Do I know you?"

"Not yet you don't, but you ain't never gonna forget me when I get finished with you!"

"Can't we reason together like sensible men?" asked the preacher.

Buck cursed, "This ain't no reasonable matter! Now you get off that horse or I'm gona yank you off."

Without another word Beecher Anderson dismounted. Once he was on the ground, Buck saw that he was a fair-sized man, maybe six feet tall. Buck himself was over six feet and weighed almost 200 pounds. He could whip any man in the settlement and did so, on a fairly regular basis.

"Put up your fists!" Buck ordered.

The preacher looked at Buck as if he was looking at a child. "Won't you just tell me what I've done to cause all of this?" he asked.

Buck started sputtering, "My wife is Mary Elms Miller. She came to hear your preaching in Georgiana yesterday. Now she's turned against me! She says she's going to leave me. It's your fault this has happened, and I aim to make you pay for it."

Buck took a swing at him but the preacher back stepped, and Buck's fist sailed harmlessly through the air. "Brother, would you mind if I take my coat off before we fight?" the preacher asked. "You see my sweet wife worked long and hard sewing this coat by lamp light. Why I treasure it almost as much as my Bible."

Buck paused and nodded his head. "Take it off!"

Buck was standing close to the preacher as he began to pull off his coat. Beecher Anderson pulled one arm out, then as the other arm came free, he hit Buck with a powerful blow. POW! It felt like a steel hammer smacking into Buck's jaw. He fell to the ground. Preacher Anderson bounced on him like a frenzied mountain lion. As he straddled Buck's chest, he delivered blow after blow—POW,POW, POW! Buck was starting to black out, but before he did, he became aware that the preacher was singing. "Oh how happy are they who the Savior obey..." It seemed as if his tormentor's fists were keeping time to the rhythm of the song. Then darkness overcame Buck.

When Buck came to, Beecher Anderson was still sitting on his chest singing like a mockingbird. Buck managed to pull one hand up into the air. "I give up preacher. You've whipped me."

The preacher looked down at Buck with an angelic smile. "Mary Elms told me about you Buck Miller. She loves you mightily, you know. I'll be coming back through this way in a few weeks to hold a longer meeting. If I let you up, I want you to give me your solemn vow that you'll come to my meetings every day along with Mary Elms and the children."

"Now wait a minute..." Buck started to say more but Beecher Anderson stopped him. "If you don't give me your word Buck, I'll just have to keep beating you till you do." With that the preacher started to sing and his fist hit Buck. POW!

"Wait!" Buck yelled. "All right, I'll do it."

"You give me your solemn word?"

"Yes. I give you my solemn word."

Preacher Anderson climbed off Buck Miller's chest. When he got to his feet he extended a hand to Buck, and helped him to his feet. Buck watched as the preacher put his coat back on.

"You better wash your face off in the creek Buck, you look pretty bad," he said. "I think you ought to apologize to your darling wife when you get back home. Good women are rare, you know. They're one of God's blessings in this life."

After Buck washed his face in the cool waters of Pigeon Creek, he and Preacher Anderson talked for awhile before the preacher went on his way. Buck asked, "Would ya mind too much not talkin' about this fight when you come back to Georgiana? I'd sure appreciate it if you wouldn't say nothin'. I'd look pretty bad in the eyes of some of my friends if they learned a preacher beat me up."

"Don't worry Buck." The preacher smiled, "I won't say a word to anyone, I surely understand! See ya in a few weeks."

Buck waved his hand as Preacher Anderson rode away singing, "Oh how happy are they who the Savior obey..."

Mary Elms never knew the reason Buck's face was so swollen when he finally came back home that day. She hugged him when he apologized to her. "Oh Buck," she said, "don't you know I would never leave you? I love you too much."

Buck Miller kept his word. He went to the meeting every day when Preacher Anderson returned to Georgiana. In fact the whole family went all four days. Buck got so he sang the hymns with gusto. He even clapped his hands. Everyone was amazed, especially Will Cranshaw.

Beecher Anderson held a baptizing on Pigeon Creek before he left the Georgiana settlement. Will and Buck got baptized along with some other folks. When Buck came up out of the water he could hear Mary Elms shouting, "Glory...glory...glory!" It was quite a day of celebration, complete with dinner served on the banks of the Pigeon Creek. Buck Miller was a changed man for, in the words of Preacher Anderson, "the gaul of bitterness' fell away from him, and the bonds of iniquity were snapped in half."

After Buck washed his face in the cool waters of Pigeon Creek, he and Preacher Anderson talked for awhile before the preacher went on his way. Buck asked, "Would ya mind too much not talkin' about this fight when you come back to Georgiana? I'd sure appreciate it if you wouldn't say nothin'. I'd look pretty bad in the eyes of some of my friends if they learned a preacher beat me up."

Sally Carter's Story

Madison County, Alabama

Many years ago, Mr. Stephen Ewing owned a large plantation called Cedarhurst. The plantation was on the corner of Whitesburg and Drake in Huntsville, Alabama. Mr. Ewing chose the name Cedarhurst because of the beautiful cedar trees that lined the driveway leading to the main house.

In 1837, Sally Carter, the beautiful 16-year-old sister of Mary Carter Ewing, Stephen's wife, became a guest at Cedarhurst. Sally was young and vibrant. She had looked forward to visiting with her sister and her family, and the social whirl of Huntsville. But shortly after Sally's arrival, she took ill and died. She was buried in the Cedarhurst cemetery.

Diseases struck quickly in the 1800s and little could be done in the way of medicines to stop the ravaging effects of harsh illnesses. Only the strongest survived. Not too long after Sally Carter's death, the Ewing's three daughter's came down with whooping cough and died. All were buried in Cedarhurst cemetery.

Then in 1865, Mary Carter Ewing passed away, and after her burial Stephen Ewing sold Cedarhusrt to Mr. Robert C. Brickell. The following 55 years brought many different owners to the plantation: the Doyles, the Tardies, the Davises, the Hughes, and the Gwins. Many of these families lived a peaceful existence at Cedarhurst.

But others were haunted by the ghost of Sally Carter.

Sally made her first appearance while the Davis family was living there. The Davises had a guest at the time. It was a young woman who was occupying an upstairs bedroom. One day, as the young guest was brushing her hair in front of the bedroom mirror she heard someone coming up the stairs. Then she heard footsteps coming down the hall toward her room. She called, "Mattie?" Mattie Davis answered from the parlor down below. At that moment, the bedroom door swung open. But no one was there. The young woman ran from the room in panic.

When she reached the parlor, Miss Mattie asked, "What's wrong?" The guest told about hearing footsteps and the door swinging open. Miss Mattie laughed and said, "Oh, don't worry, its only Sally Carter. She does that sometimes. She won't hurt you."

When the J.D. Thornton family bought Cedarhurst in 1919, Mrs. Thornton's 17-year-old cousin, Charles Roland, came to visit from Dothan. At the time, the Thorntons were holding a family reunion and every bedroom in the house was filled. Charles ended up on a cot in the hall just outside the room where Sally Carter had died so many years before.

A storm came up one night and there was thunder and lightning. A hard wind howled among the trees outside. The next morning the storm was gone and in its place was sunshine. The family and guests gathered for a large breakfast, but Charles Roland failed to join them. Finally, Mrs. Thornton went to look for him. She found Charles sitting on the front porch. He was wet and disheveled and literally shaking all over.

Charles Roland had experienced a nightmare encounter with Sally Carter. She had even spoken to Charles, explaining exactly who she was. In a soft voice she said, "The storm has blown my tombstone over, will you please come and place it upright again? I can't bear for it to lie on the ground!" Charles then told how Sally took him by his arm, pulling him down the stairs and out across the yard. He managed to pull away, tried to come back inside the house, but found all the doors locked.

Another Thornton guest experienced Sally's ghost too. He was actually a boarder in the Thornton home. This fellow slept in Sally's old bedroom. He was a heavy cigarette smoker, and kept finding ashtrays dumped onto the floor with ashes scattered. Finally one evening he heard a young woman's voice say, "Really sir, smoking is such a horrible habit. If you must smoke, please do so outside."

The boarder continued to smoke, but never again in the house. This man told about not being able to keep his bedroom door locked. "Everytime I lock the door," he said, "some unseen hand unlocks it!"

A developer bought the Cedarhurst property in the 1980s, built a residential area and used the old mansion as the clubhouse. The developer decided to move the cemetery, and when the vaults were dug up, only four were recovered. The vault of Sally Carter was never found.

In 1985, Decorator's Showplace featured the Cedarhurst Clubhouse. The old mansion had been restored to its former grandeur, and was open to the public for about two weeks. During the second week, there were unexplainable mishaps in Sally Carter's bedroom. The room had been decorated for a teen-age girl with blue and peach bows, silk flowers—even a personal diary. It looked beautiful, yet one morning a floral bouquet was found overturned on the floor. Days later, the bedroom was found in shambles: the diary lay open on the floor, the silk flowers were scattered about, bedcovers lay wadded in a heap in the middle of the bed. No one knows exactly what happened that night. What they do know is that the house had been straightened up and securely locked the evening before. No locks or win-

dows were broken, and it appeared that whoever tore up Sally's room was already in the house.

Many overnight guests staying in the Cedarhurst guest house spoke of hearing strange footsteps. They told of doors opening and closing all hours of the night. The ghost of Sally Carter lives on in the minds and imaginations of Huntsville citizens. It has been this way since her death 160 years ago. Her tombstone has suffered over the years, as thrill seekers come and chip away pieces of the stone for souvenirs. Perhaps someday Sally will find peace.

Her epitaph reads:
My flesh shall slumber in the ground,
Till the last trumpet's joyful sound.
Then burst the chains with sweet surprise,
And in my savior's image rise.

This story was contributed by: Sara Wattenbarger McDaris. Sara has served as a Huntsville Public Librarian since 1976. She was the producer, storyteller and host of "Grunches And Grins," aired on Alabama Public Television from 1972-1992. Sara was the first regional representative from the State of Alabama to tell stories at the National Storytelling Festival in Jonesborough, Tennessee in 1976.

Sally took him by his arm, pulling him down the stairs and out across the yard. He managed to pull away, tried to come back inside the house, but found all the doors locked.

Birmingham's Mystic Underground River

Jefferson County, Alabama

In the early days of Fort Jonesborough, in 1813, Indians came to trade with the settlers. When these native people came to trade, their children often ran and played with the settler's children. Sometimes the children would brag to one another about the speed of their ponies, or the intelligence of their dogs and wolf puppies. Sometimes the Indian children would say, "We came from the north in canoes, along the beautiful underground river. It has always been used by our people."

"Where is it?" the settler's children would ask.

"Not far from here," they would reply.

In later years, after Birmingham became a city, the underground river was discovered by its residents. The river's current flowed swiftly, especially after hard rains when its original source filled with fresh water. One access to the river was found by entering a cave near Highland Avenue and 12th street. Many older residents have a knowledge of this old cave. Some of them have seen the river, and watched its blue waters flow majestically through the underground channel. City officials must have feared someone would drown, for they sealed the Highland

Avenue entrance in the early 1900s.

In the late 1880s and early 1890s there was an office in a building somewhere around Fifth Avenue and 22nd Street North where tickets could be purchased for a tour of the "Mystic Underground River."

A few residents remember hearing relatives say that the underground river surfaced as a spring at 5th Avenue and 22nd Street. They say that for many years this spring was a welcome source of clean drinking water for Birmingham residents. Eventually though, the spring dried up, but the underground river continued to flow.

Residents in the Bessemer area tell of going into caves and observing the river. People in Trussville tell the same stories. One man said he believes the river flows from Tennessee to Jefferson County. He said, "I heard of a man up in Tennessee who found a large source of underground water flowing. He made up a big batch of cement and poured it into the water and do you know, a few weeks later some fellows in Bessemer found large amounts of cement in the underground river here!"

Another man told of a special type of albino catfish that can be caught in the "Mystic River." He said, "My granddaddy used to catch 'em. They were big catfish too. Granddaddy would fry up these fine catfish steaks, they were just as sweet tastin' as honey." When asked if he had ever seen the river he said, "I saw it once when I was just a little boy."

It's a fact that when the Tutwiler Hotel was built in 1913, workmen dug right through the ceiling of the underground river. They could see the water rushing past. Building plans were halted on the hotel until it was decided to use steel beams and crisscross them forming a bridge over the river. This bridge was part of the Tutwiler's foundation.

Other city buildings have been affected by the river too. The Florentine Club, built at Second Avenue North and 22nd Street; the Federal Reserve Bank at Fifth Avenue and 18th Street; the Daniel Building on 20th Street; and last but not least, the Birmingham-Jefferson Civic Center. One lady says the underground river is visible from the bottom of the Civic Center and she has seen it there.

Historians have recorded that there was a time when several buildings along the course of the river sank wells into it for use as an inexpensive water source for heating and air conditioning.

Many people have contributed to this story. Thanks to The Birmingham News *article printed in 1975.*

Bugaboo Mountain Tales

Near Andrews Chapel, West Morgan County, Alabama

Haunting, unexplainable tales involving Bugaboo Mountain have been told since before the Civil War. Even the word, Bugaboo, infers mystery. It means an imaginary object arousing fear and distress. People who live near the mountain will tell you the name fits. There are many stories connected to Bugaboo Mountain. Here are two of them.

Freedom Money

On many nights during the year, a light can be seen moving around on Bugaboo Mountain. No one seems to know for sure why the light shines, but some people believe it is the spirit of ole' Mose, a slave who once lived on a farm adjoining the mountain.

Mose was not his real name. Only the winds of Africa know his real name, but here he was called Mose, and he was the slave of John Hunter.

Mose was dependable and extremely hard working. So much so that Mr. Hunter allowed him special privileges. Mose and his wife, Annie, lived apart from the other slaves in a four-room log cabin. When their chores were finished, they had six acres they could farm for themselves. Annie sewed clothes and quilts by hand, and when Mose wasn't farming, they made white oak baskets in every shape and size.

On Saturdays, Mr. Hunter arranged for Mose and Annie to take their goods into town. They sold them in the local market, and were allowed to keep the money they earned. Ole' Mose buried it in a secret place on Bugaboo Mountain. A place that only he knew about.

Mose had a fire for freedom burning in his heart, freedom for himself and Annie. So one day he asked Mr. Hunter if he might buy their freedom when they had enough money. A price was set, and bit by bit, year by year the freedom money grew.

Then one spring day, when Annie's flowers were starting to bloom, Mose told her they had enough money to pay Mr. Hunter's price. The two of them sat up late that night, talking, planning, even dancing for joy!

But something terrible happened that night. Five mean, lawless men, thirsting for easy money, rode to Mose and Annie's cabin. They kicked down the door, demanding to know where the money was hidden. When Mose refused to tell, they tied him up and carried him away. Poor Annie ran for help.

They found ole' Mose's body on Bugaboo Mountain. Several fingers were missing from his lifeless hands.

Mose was buried on the Hunter farm, and Annie was given her freedom. She lived out her life in the four room log cabin. None of the men who committed the murder were ever caught.

A light appeared on Bugaboo Mountain about a month after Mose died. It moved around all over the mountainside. It has been shining ever since. Some people say the light is ole' Mose wandering about on the mountain. They say his spirit still guards the Freedom Money.

Ghost Wagons

Joe Hamilton's hounds barked and pulled against the ropes that held them to the Sweet Gum tree. He glanced back at them as he rode his horse into the darkness toward Bugaboo Mountain.

It had been exactly two weeks since that night the dogs started barking, and took off up the mountain. This evening, Joe decided to follow them. He wanted to see what was upsetting them. Joe rode his horse up the mountain as far as the rock formations. When he reined the horse in, he sat listening as the hounds continued to bark and bay. Then Joe heard another sound. It was the sound of wheel axles squeaking, and a chill passed down the back of his neck because he was certain he knew what the sound meant!

Joe remembered his grandpa Hamilton telling him stories when he was little. Stories about invisible wagons that rolled endlessly across Bugaboo Mountain. Grandpa and his friends chased after the wagon sounds when they were young. "Sometimes," grandpa said, "those wheels were so close we could reach out and touch them. Then the sounds would stop, and we couldn't find a trace of wagon tracks or bent bushes." Joe's father always said grandpa's stories were nonsense. Just an old man's tales. Still, Joe listened and wondered.

During all these years, Joe had never heard the sounds until now. Sitting on his horse in the darkness, he clearly heard the creaking sounds of wagon wheels crunching over rocks and sticks. They were passing somewhere just below him.

Joe kicked his horse and rode toward the sounds. When he found his dogs, they were whining and sniffing the ground. Joe took them back home. Then he got his sleeping bag and a flashlight and rode back up the mountain to see if he could solve the mystery.

As he started up the incline, he again heard the wagons. He tried to hurry his horse by slapping it with the reins, but the trail was slippery with pine needles and loose rock. The horse kept stumbling. Finally Joe shouted, "Wait! I want to talk to you." The noise ceased. For a while, Hamilton sat there listening. Finally he dismounted and unrolled his sleeping bag.

Sometime in the early morning hours he roused from his sleep. Hamilton sat bolt upright, hardly daring to breathe. He not only heard wagons rolling past him, he heard horses snorting and a cow mooing! A full moon was shining as Joe pulled on his boots and hurried after the sounds. He never reached them.

When he returned home the next morning, Hamilton untied his hounds. He knew eventually they would tire of chasing phantom noises. As for himself, he never intended to look for the wagons again. He decided whoever or whatever it was, he would leave them alone to make their invisible journey as long as was necessary.

Years later Joe Hamilton told his grandchildren about the wagons on Bugaboo Mountain. His son didn't believe him. He called it nonsense...an old man's tale.

Those who know the story about the invisible wagons speculate when and what started the strange sounds that are heard on Bugaboo Mountain even today. Some people say they were wagons driven by a Union cannon crew lost from their regiment during the Civil War. Other's believe the sounds predate that war. They say the wagons belonged to early Alabama settlers bound from Tennessee. Perhaps they met with yellow fever, malaria or sleeping sickness. Maybe it was a combination of the three. According to old writings, mosquitoes were "thick as gnats, and big as hummingbirds."

Regardless, wagon by wagon, those who crossed Bugaboo Mountain may have taken sick as home remedies failed and fever spread like a dry wood's fire. Some managed to continue, while others—entire families—may have perished on the mountain. Is it possible that somehow they spend the centuries rolling across that haunted mountain, trying in vain to free themselves?

Sources: *An article by Brooks Bolick, reporter for the* Decatur Daily, *1985. Mr. Bolick credited Bob Woodruff, Louie & Otis Dutton, and Pauline Gibson with the stories. Both stories have been adapted.*

Fetching Henry Home

Russell County, Alabama

Henry Gains left this life on January 20, 1829, as the result of a brawl in a tavern. This tavern was in the small community of Sodom, present day Phoenix City in Russell County. At the time, Henry was fighting with a group of ruffians when one of the them picked up a large stone and smacked him 'side o' the head,' splitting it like a watermelon. A friend of Henry Gains, one Samuel Carpenter, was with him at the time of the incident. Samuel, realizing Henry was dead, searched through his jacket and found a considerable sum of money. He took Henry's money, and made immediate arrangements with a local carpenter to build him a coffin. The body was placed into the coffin, and it was nailed shut.

The next morning Mr. Carpenter paid a stage driver the remainder of Henry Gains's money to ship the coffin to Montgomery where the Gains family lived. Mr. Carpenter also paid for a seat on the stage.

A party of three passengers from Georgia had been traveling on this mail stage. There were two gentlemen and a rather large maiden lady named Elizabeth Blann. Miss Blann was traveling with her cousin, Mr. George Vick. She was moving from Georgia to Montgomery to live with a different set of relatives. The matter of Henry Gaines's coffin caused a critical problem for the passengers.

Stage drivers were often a rowdy, arrogant bunch. They considered themselves *Kings of the Road* wielding more power than the staunchest sea captain. When the stage driver accepted payment to ship Henry's coffin, he gave the other passengers the ultimatum of continuing their journey or waiting for the next stage. They knew he meant it. No one was certain when or if another stage would pass through Sodom. When they asked the stage driver, he shrugged his shoulders and replied, "Might be a few days. Might be a few weeks. Might be a few months." Miss Blann burst into tears. So the passengers decided to continue in spite of Henry Gains.

The trip from Sodom to Montgomery was not that far, but travel in those days was different from today. Roads, at best, were rough and the fastest mileage they could make was about four or five miles an hour. Relay stations were 12 to 14 miles apart. The trip could take several days. January was producing unseasonably strong winds, rain, sleet and snow that year. The air was freezing, which was one reason Samuel Carpenter decided to take Henry Gains home. He felt certain the corpse would stay in good condition until the family could arrange the burial.

When the stagecoach pulled away that morning, luggage, mail and other shippable items rode topside with the driver while the coffin was in the coach, protruding out windows on either side. (Coffins were built different at the time, they were much narrower than they are today.) It was strapped down to rings in the coach floor.

One male passenger and Mr. Carpenter took a seat with their backs to the upcoming road while Miss Blann and Mr. Vick rode facing forward, though wedged into their seat by the coffin. I might add that Miss Blann was wedged very tightly. The driver shouted, cracking his whip and the stagecoach lunged forward. The coffin bounced against its ropes.

Rain poured down all morning. The wind, thunder

and lightning took turns blowing, flashing, and booming as the road slowly filled with water. They had not traveled far when Miss Blann suddenly took it into her head that the corpse was moving and thrashing about in the box. Her eyes grew wide with fear as she screamed above the outside noises, "It's alive!" Her coach companions, lost in their thoughts, almost jumped out of their skins!

Elizabeth Blann's head was rotating from side to side. Her eyeballs rolled wildly as she shoved against the coffin with both hands trying to free herself from the wedge. The entire time she continued to scream, "It's alive, it's alive!" A hysterical woman has a profoundly unnerving effect on even the strongest male. All the gentlemen sat there as if frozen to their seats, staring at Henry Gains' coffin. It was moving. But then everyone in the coach was bouncing around. Besides, the man had been dead almost 24 hours and it was a certainty he could not budge. They each took turns trying to tell Miss Blann this, but she was wailing louder than the wind and would not be comforted. The rising rain waters eventually slowed the stage's progress, which proved to be a blessing, because the coffin did not move as much. Miss Blann slowly managed to calm herself, and finally fell asleep.

The stage eventually reached a Creek Indian encampment near a large swamp. A bridge of sorts went over some of the bog. It was the first of many such bridges spanning the swamp. These were crude bridges, some fairly high, covered with rough planks and no railings. When the coach stopped, all the male passengers got off, leaving Miss Blann asleep in her seat. She was bent forward with her head resting on the coffin.

When the journey resumed, there was an additional passenger—a rather large, lanky, old Creek. His head was wrapped in a turban and he wore a bright blue shirt and had silver ornaments and shells around his neck. He also wore tight-fitting buckskin pants. His gray hair hung down from under the turban. He paid the stage driver several gold coins for his seat. Miss Blann's cousin gladly gave the newcomer his place and moved between Mr. Carpenter and the other passenger. The old Creek glanced at Elizabeth Blann as she snored gently in her troubled sleep.

The stage rolled away without mishap. The winds slowly decreased as the rain became a light drizzle. Everything went well until they got half-way across the fourth bridge. Miss Elizabeth woke up. She must have been dreaming for she had a trance-like expression on her face as she shouted, "It's alive!" She began pounding the coffin with both fists. The old warrior had drifted off to sleep, but the shock of Miss Blann's actions woke him, and he whipped out a large, wicked looking knife that was concealed under his shirt. It was a reflex.

Miss Blann was not even aware that the Indian was sitting beside her until he whipped out his knife. When she saw him and the blade, her screams mounted the air like a hurricane. She turned her terrified wrath from the coffin to the old warrior, and he let out a blood chilling war whoop! All three gentlemen passengers, sensing grave danger, touched their scalps and began shouting. The stage came to an abrupt halt just as it reached the far side of the bridge and rolled onto solid ground. The driver swung down and yanked the coach door open, thus abating what might have been a terrible scene.

Once they all calmed down, Miss Blann insisted the five men open Henry Gains' coffin. When they did, they peered down on poor Henry.

And to their frightened amazement, his eyes opened and Henry stared right back at them.

Poor Henry, they discovered at that moment, was very much alive. Thank God, Mr. Carpenter had not buried him in Sodom. Thank God, Miss Elizabeth was given to hysteria.

The old Creek carried a packet of herbal powder. He sprinkled the powder onto Henry's wound, and the men bandaged his head with a piece of Elizabeth Blann's petticoat. Miss Blann gave Henry two dried biscuits she had in her purse. He rode beside her, the remainder of the trip, at first resting his weary head on her shoulder.

They made two overnight stops in stage houses along the way, but I'm happy to say the coach reached Montgomery without further incident. Everyone was reasonably comfortable after they dumped the coffin. Once they arrived in Montgomery, the passengers went their separate ways.

Henry Gains changed his habits for the better after his ordeal. The Gains family knew the family of Miss Blann. Henry was so grateful to Elizabeth for saving his life that he began visiting with her on a regular basis. They fell in love and were married the following Christmas.

This tale is based on Alabama History and a fact taken from a story an elderly woman shared with me many years ago. At the time I met her, this lady was living in a nursing home in downtown Birmingham. I had gone there to share stories with the residents, and when I finished she said, "Now I have some stories I want to share with you." That was almost thirty years ago. I can still picture the woman in my mind, but I do not know her name.

Funeral Home Tales

Jefferson County, Alabama

The Accident

Late one warm, rainy Sunday afternoon in 1952 a gray two-door Plymouth sedan made its way down the street in front of Elmwood Cemetery. Mrs. Lou Perkins was on her way home from a church service. She gripped the wheel tightly, as she was uneasy when it was raining. Lou's eyesight wasn't as good as it had once been, and there was the possibility the car might slid on the wet pavement. The rain increased, and Lou wished she had stayed home. She was thinking about *Tink*, her little dog, when she suddenly slammed on the brakes. Lou Perkins screamed as the Plymouth began to slide toward the edge of the pavement. It crashed into a ditch.

Billy Eubanks was coming in the opposite direction when he saw the gray Plymouth run off the road. He could see the fear on the old woman's face, as he watched the car plunge down into the ditch. Eubanks quickly pulled to the side of the road, jumped out of his car and ran over to see if the woman was hurt. Several other cars had pulled off by the time he got there.

"What happened?" one of the drivers asked?

Billy Eubanks answered, "I don't know, she just seemed to lose control of her car."

When they opened the driver's door, Lou was crying. "Are you all right?" They asked.

Her hands were shaking, but she nodded her head and said, "Yes, I'm all right, but what about that poor woman I hit! Oh my God! I've killed someone!"

"What woman?" Billy Eubanks said as he looked toward the road. "You didn't hit anyone," he assured her.

She leaned forward staring out at the road, then she looked at them with disbelief. "But she was there—right in front of my car. A blond woman in a dark brown raincoat. I tried to stop! It just happened so quickly."

Billy Eubanks studied the road for a moment, "Lady, there's no one out there. You must have just thought you saw someone."

As they were talking, a police car pulled up, and two officers walked over to Lou Perkins car. She was still convinced that she had hit someone on the road. The officers had a strange look on their faces. One of them walked back to the squad car and clicked on his police radio. "I have a one car accident," he reported. "Yeah. It's an elderly lady. She's run off the road. Lost control. Did Phillips call in? They have him? Okay." He clicked off the radio and walked back to Lou's car.

"I've called a wrecker ma'am. They should be here in a few minutes. You want us to take you by the hospital? You should let them check you over to make sure you're all right."

"I'm not hurt," she answered. "I'm just upset and confused. I saw someone in the road. I thought I hit her."

The other officer had walked out to the road. When he came back he said, "Ma'am, you didn't hit anyone." Then the officers shared some information with Lou and the individuals standing around her car. It was information about another accident that had occurred a few blocks down the street.

Days later Lou Eubanks was talking with her friend Ida Mae Chappel. She was trying to tell Ida Mae what had happened. "It's the strangest thing Ida Mae, I was going right past Elmwood Cemetery in the rain, and I was thinking about little *Tink*. My mind drifted for a few seconds till all of a sudden I saw this woman in front of my car with her hands up as if she was trying to get me to stop. Well, I hit my brakes, but I couldn't stop on that slick pavement. I hit her. Then I lost control, and my car slid right off the road. That's all I remember untill those young men opened my car door."

A woman was hit the same day Lou Eubanks had her accident. It happened exactly two blocks further down the street from Elmwood Cemetery. She was crossing the street when a car, driven by a hit and run driver, killed her. However, the woman wasn't a blond. She was a brunette, and she wasn't wearing a dark brown raincoat. She was wearing a white dress. It could have been Lou Perkins driving the fatal car that day, but someone stopped Lou, minutes ahead of the other accident.

A Day In Old Birmingham

When Birmingham was a young city, back around 1895, a happy undertaker owned a small business nestled between a general mercantile and another shop on 20th Street. Mind you, things were different back then—yet human behavior rarely, if ever, changes all that much.

Driggers was the proprietor's name, Gregory J. Driggers. He was an excellent artisan who understood the importance of his craft. There was nothing conspicuous about Mr. Drigger's business. He felt that would be in poor taste. Besides, he relied on satisfied customers. The families he served always sent him new clients as the need arose. The front window of Mr. Drigger's shop was plain, containing blue curtains which framed the words:

GREGORY J. DRIGGERS

"Here To Serve Your Loved Ones"

One cool, fall morning, a handsome young man with brown, disheveled hair walked into Mr. Driggers shop. This young fellow's eyes were red and puffy, his clothing wrinkled. Otherwise he looked fairly well. Mr. Driggers, professional that he was, immediately recognized a man in grief.

He greeted the young gentleman in his most tender voice, "Good morning sir, may I assist you?"

A smile broke over the young man's face, "I sure hope so," he replied.

Mr. Driggers noted the smile. "A relative?" he asked.

Another broad smile covered the young man's face, "Yes sir, my wife!"

Mr. Driggers studied him for a moment. "Sorry," he says. "Was it sudden?"

"Sudden? I should say not. I've never seen anything take so long in my whole life. I always thought it would happen quickly."

Mr. Driggers thought, 'Odd reply—oh well, grief affects everyone in a different way.' "Have you considered a price?" he asked.

The young man was thoughtful. "Well, I suppose about 'middle-of-the-road' would be good. I want it to look good, but I'm not a rich man either."

Mr. Driggers nodding his head asked, "Have you decided what color satin you would like?"

The young man looked puzzled, "Satin?" he asked.

"Yes," said Driggers, "We always line them with satin."

"I suppose I can understand that," said the young fellow, "it should be soft against their skin, though I doubt they notice it much." He laughed.

Mr. Driggers cleared his throat. "Most people choose white satin," he stated.

"That'll be fine," replied the young man.

In almost a whisper Mr. Driggers asked, "Would you like metal handles on it? Again there was a puzzled expression on the young gentleman's face. "I suppose," he said, "but I only need one handle on it."

Driggers was writing everything down in his order book. He looked up and said, "One? Surely you need two, sir. How will you left her?"

The young patron smiled, "If I wanted to lift her, I suppose I'd just pick her up. She ain't that heavy, you know?"

Mr. Driggers frowned and thought again it was an odd reply.

"It will have wheels, won't it?" the young man asked.

"Wheels?" asked Mr. Driggers, raising his eyebrows a bit.

"Sure! It will be easy rolling her around then."

Mr. Driggers was beginning to feel uneasy with the conversation. He couldn't help thinking that this young man might not be as "together" as he had first appeared. "Why would you want to roll her around?" he asked.

"Why, so's everybody in the neighborhood can have a look at her of course!"

Mr. Driggers backed away from his customer a few steps. Frowning again, he rolled his tongue over his lips.

The last remark had truly startled him, but he quickly composed himself. Replying in a much firmer voice he said, "Sir, won't they view her at your home?"

The young fellow looked thoughtful, "Not all of them," he replied. "Besides, I think I'll enjoy rolling her around a bit."

This was too much! Roll her around, indeed. "Sir! Don't you plan to bury her?"

"Bury her?" Now it was the young man's turn to look startled. He leaned forward and said, "Are you crazy? What kind of talk is that? I want her with me, not in the ground! Grant you, I may wish I had buried her after a while, but right now I intend to have some fun with her."

Driggers was completely alarmed. He looked at the window to see if an officer of the peace might be in sight. This young man had bats in his belfry! Gently—very gently he said, "But sir, no one rolls a coffin."

"A coffin! What'cha talkin' about? I don't want no coffin! I come in here to buy a carriage for my baby girl!"

Mr. Driggers's jaw gaped open. "A carriage?"

The young man replied, "Sure."

Mr. Driggers pulled himself up as straight as he could and announced, "Sir, I run a funeral parlor!"

Now it was the young gentleman's jaw that gaped open. "A funeral parlor!"

"Yes sir. I sell coffins."

The young man's face was turning red, "This ain't the General Mercantile?"

"No sir." Mr. Driggers pointed as he spoke. "That would be next door."

Such tales as these are shared by those who work in Funeral Homes in the Birmingham area.

Undertaker: "Sir! Don't you plan to bury her?"

"Bury her? Are you crazy? What kind of talk is that? I want her with me, not in the ground! Grant you, I may wish I had buried her after a while, but right now I intend to have some fun with her."

How the Hen Got Baptized

Walker County, Alabama

Jackson Daniels preached at Shady Grove Baptist Church near Jasper, for more than 15 years. When he was nearing his 67th birthday, the deacons came to him saying that many people in the congregation wanted a younger man. Someone who could better relate to the young people. The deacons pointed out, "Your sermons have grown stale, and you repeat them too often." Preacher Daniels knew this was true. He had become stagnant; fervor was hard to find. He spent much of his time caring for Melissa, his wife of more than 40 years. She had been ill for quite a while.

On Friday evening the following week, the deacons held a second meeting. After it was over, Preacher Daniels went into the church. Kneeling, he began to pray earnestly, explaining his situation to the Lord and beseeching Him for inspiration. Afterward, he walked into his study and proceeded to write one of the best sermons he had composed in many years.

That Sunday morning in May 1920, the congregation noticed the baptistry curtains drawn open. They wondered about it as there was no announcement of a baptizing. Preacher Daniel's sermon would deal with life that morning. It would deal with human struggles, new beginnings, and a new start. The baptistry was a visual to emphasize the message. When the singing ended, he launched into his sermon, immediately capturing the congregation's attention. The tempo began a steady climb. The sermon was inspired.

No one ever knew just where the hen came from. The church doors were closed but down the aisle she came—a fat, reddish brown hen. She walked as though she had just stepped into a fox's den. She raised one scrawny leg high in the air and placed it carefully in front of the other. Her neck was outstretched. Her head turned from one side to the other, her eyes blinking. At first Preacher Daniels didn't notice. In fact, no one noticed. Of course by the time the thing reached mid church, many eyes were locked onto it including those of several deacons. At that very moment Preacher Daniels hit the high point of his sermon. Determined to strike a deep chord and rouse slumbering souls, he shouted, his fist pounding the pulpit. The noise caused the hen to jump straight up, cackling and flapping her wings in terror.

The children loved it. Several climbed on the pews, pointing, as embarrassed mothers struggled to seat them. A ripple of laughter spread through the congregation.

Preacher Daniel's fist hung suspended in midair, his eyes frozen on the wayward chicken. Brother Simpson, a deacon seated near the back, left his pew. He started down the aisle running, hands outstretched as though to strangle her. The hen took wing when she spotted him and fluttered over Mrs. Bean and her six children. Mrs. Bean commenced screaming like a banshee, flaying her arms wildly while running in a stationary position.

At that point, pandemonium broke loose. Everyone was trying to capture the hen. It flew. It ducked. And it finally managed to reach the altar area. Preacher Daniel's face was livid. He had passed through several emotional phases since first making eye contact with the hen. Here he was, preaching on borrowed time, desperately needing to connect with his congregation, and now it was out of control. He could even hear cursing. By this time there were five men in the altar area, three deacons and two helpers. Something deep inside Preacher Daniels snapped and he forsook the pulpit. The hen was running towards him and he threw the hymnal at it. He not only threw the hymnal, but he also threw the Holy Bible at it! When this happened, a woman on the front row fainted.

Four more good brothers mounted the altar area. Brother Simpson and Brother Quinn leaped headlong at the same time. The hen flew straight up, and the deacons heads "bammed" together like fighting mountain goats.

This time the hen stayed airborne. Up, up she flew. The glass on the baptistry was open halfway up and the hen flew over it, hitting the water with a loud SPLASH. Everyone froze until little Bobby Grant, nine-year-old grandson of Deacon Simpson, shouted, "Look! She's baptized herself." Laughter immediately erupted all over the church. Even Preacher Daniels was laughing.

They fished the poor hen out, dried her with a towel and escorted her safely out of the church. Preacher Daniels finished his sermon on a much lighter note. Three people came forward when the "call" was given. That was more than had come in many months.

Preacher Daniels continued to preach at Shady Grove for several more years. He is well remembered in that church. Of course the hen is remembered too. Who would ever forget the day the hen got baptized!

This story was adapted from a tale my dear neighbor, Mrs. Bonnie Hollingsworth, now deceased, shared with me many years ago in Homewood. Names, church and exact location have been changed to protect the innocent— everyone except the hen.

Jessie

DeKalb County, Alabama

A long time ago, not far from Buck's Pocket, there once lived a man with his wife, son, and little girl. I've been told the little girl's name was "Jessie." She was twelve years old, and had the blackest hair you ever saw. Black as a crow's wing. Black as a moonless midnight sky.

Jessie was a happy child, always laughing and smiling. She was a pleasure to be around.

One morning when Jessie woke up her mama was bending over her bed with her face close to Jessie's face. Her mama whispered, "Come on Jessie, get up. Hurry and get yourself dressed, 'cause we're going across the valley to visit with our kinfolks today."

Jessie's mother had sisters who lived across the valley, up on the ridges of the next mountain. Normally, Jessie would have jumped at the chance to make a trip, but for whatever reason, she begged to stay home that day.

"Aw mama, I don't want to go. Please let me stay home this time."

Her mama looked shocked as she answered, "Now Jessie, you know I can't leave you home alone. You're too young to stay by yourself. Besides, we'll be gone till day after tomorrow most likely."

"But mama, I'll do just fine. I'm 12 years old now. I

know how to cook, and how to take care of myself. Besides, you know ol' Mob's not about to let anything happen to me."

Mob was Jessie's big, cream-colored dog. She had raised him from a tiny pup that used to fit into the palm of her hand. Mob loved Jessie better than his life. Jessie kept right on begging until her mother finally agreed to leave her behind.

When the family left in the wagon that day, Jessie was standing on the wooden porch waving goodbye to them. Mob stood beside her wagging his tail. After the wagon passed out of sight down the long rocky road, Jessie turned and walked into the house.

She set about getting all the chores done. First Jessie made the beds, and then she washed up the dishes. Next Jessie brought fresh water in from the well, fed the chickens, and gathered the eggs. Then she milked the cow, and hoed the weeds in the vegetable garden just like her mama always did. By the time evening set in, Jessie had finished with everything.

The sun was going down as she washed up her supper dishes and put them away. Jessie started a fire in the fireplace, then sat down in front of it. Taking her needlework in her lap, she sewed on a cross-stitch piece that showed a schoolhouse in the springtime when all the pretty wildflowers were blooming.

Jessie could hear the wind as it gently passed through the pine trees outside. She rocked as she sewed, and ol' Mob slept quietly at her feet. Jessie was humming a little tune her grandmama had taught her, when Mob began to growl. He didn't even open his eyes at first. Mob just lay there rumbling deep down in his throat. Then he jumped to his feet barking! It was so sudden, he caused Jessie to jump and miss a stitch. She said, "What is it Mob?" Jessie sat very still listening for any unusual sound, but she couldn't hear anything except the wind. Finally Mob laid back down, and she resumed her sewing.

A few more minutes passed, then Mob was on his feet

again barking wildly!

He went to the door and started pawing at it. Jessie's heart was pounding inside her chest. She set the sewing down, and walked to the door. "What is it Mob? You hear something I can't hear?"

Lifting the heavy bolt that locked the door, Jessie stepped onto the porch, holding Mob by the fur on his neck. She listened carefully as she stared out into the darkness. She figured it was a bear or something that had spooked her dog. When Jessie didn't hear anything, she turned to go back inside. Then she heard a faint sound coming up the long, rocky road that her parents had gone down earlier. It sounded like a low whistle, making first a high note, then a low note. Jessie knew it wasn't the sound of a bird. Mob jumped hard when he heard the whistle, and broke free. He ran into the yard barking.

"Mob you come back here!" Jessie called.

The big dog stopped and returned to his mistress. They went back inside the cabin and Jessie closed the door, pulling the bolt back across it. Her heart was beating loud enough for her to hear it. She tried to calm herself by believing it was just the nighttime playing tricks on her imagination. After all, she had never been alone at night and the whole experience was scary. Everything was different now that darkness had fallen.

Jessie sat in the rocker leaving her sewing on the floor. She wished her folks were there. If only she knew where her daddy kept his big gun. He hid it after cousin Rake played with it and shot mama's mirror all to smash.

Mob started barking again. He'd bark and whine, then bark again as he ran back and forth from the door to Jessie. There was a wild excitement in his eyes. Jessie could hear the whistling sound, it was getting closer to the cabin. Finally Mob was so frantic acting that she got up. Running to the door, Jessie lifted the bolt, and let the door swing open. Then she said, "Go get 'em Mob!"

The dog jumped off the porch, and ran down the road, barking as he went. Jessie stood on the porch. She listened as Mob continued through the darkness. At first she heard his paws hitting against the gravel rocks, then she heard him snarling—intent on his prey. The last sound Jessie heard was Mob yelping. Silence followed. The whistling started up again.

Jessie felt cold. She felt icy cold. She stepped back inside the cabin, and pulled the bolt down, securing the door. Then she sat down in her rocking chair. Tears trickled down her cheeks as she sat down before the fire. It glowed all red and warm, but Jessie's teeth were chattering. She crossed her arms over her chest, and tucked her hands down under her arms. She began to hum softly.

The next evening Jessie's folks arrived back home. Her mother had been too worried to stay gone as long as she had planned. Jessie's daddy knocked on the cabin door and called "Jessie. Jessie!" But no one answered. The door was locked from the inside. Finally, he went around to a tiny window in the back of the cabin. It was their only glass window. He broke the glass, and helped her brother climb through it.

Jessie's brother found her, sitting in the rocking chair, in front of a fire long grown cold. She was just sitting there, with her arms crossed, staring into the ashes and humming.

The boy unlocked the door, and let his mother and father into the cabin. When Jessie's mother saw her sitting in the rocking chair, she rushed over to her daughter's side. She began to wail, sobbing, "Jessie! Jessie! Why'd I leave you alone? Why'd I listen to you? Jessie! My poor little baby."

It was all very strange. They were never sure exactly what happened that night. They never found ol' Mob. All Jessie's daddy found was a blood track that led off into the woods. Later, he found a small reed whistle. It lay on the ground beneath the back window.

Jessie was never the same after that night she spent alone. Instead of laughing and teasing, the way she always had, she was quite and withdrawn acting. Her hair was different too. It turned completely white that night. White as a new fallen snow. Everywhere she went, for a long time, people stared at her.

We heard a variant of this tale told for truth back in 1973, during an in-service workshop on oral storytelling given for Jefferson County teachers. Many Alabama school children have also contributed to the tale over the years. Tales about people having their hair turn white from fear are commonly found among folk tales.

Levi's Gold

Hale County, Alabama

In Hale County there once lived a man named Wiggins—Levi Wiggins.

Levi lived the life of a wealthy man, yet he never planted, never harvested, never borrowed and as far as anybody knew, he never worked. He wore store-bought clothes and lived in a better than average house. His fourteen kids wore shoes—every day! Folks wondered.

Water isn't the only thing a dowsing stick can be used for; a person can go dowsing for just about anything. I suspect old Levi Wiggins was the champion dowser of them all, for he could find water on the driest desert! Most of the time Levi dowsed for much more than water. Levi Wiggins dowsed for gold.

You might wonder how in the world he knew where to search. It wasn't hard. Levi was fond of courthouse records, especially those that described abandoned property. He knew how it was in the days before ordinary people trusted banks. A family might hide its gold away in root cellars, behind wallboards, inside wells, beside oak trees, or even out in cornfields.

Whenever Levi located an old homestead gone cold from lack of family, he would pay a visit with his dowsing rod. Sooner or later, he would locate something. Most often it was gold. The government hadn't called the gold in at the time the homestead was active.

The stick never failed Levi. As soon as it located metal, it nose-dived and pointed pretty as a bird-dog. Oh, it's true, sometimes he fell into a false dig. Maybe he would dig up spoons or a watch or such, but more often than not, he would strike pure gold.

A family lived not too far from Levi Wiggins. The old ones had passed and the farm house was closed. They built another house just over the hill from the old place, and one day a grandson noticed Levi hanging around.

"Maw, Levi Wiggins is up to no good," he said. "He's hanging around grandpaw's place, and you know what he's lookin' for."

His mother didn't seem to care. "Leave him be," she answered.

Day after day Levi kept hanging around. The boy made no secret that he saw him. "I know what you're doing," he told Levi.

One night after supper, the boy was sitting on the front porch with his dog when he noticed a light crossing the road. He watched as the light wound through the woods up to the old farm. "Maw!" he shouted. "Levi Wiggins has come to dig Grandpaw's gold!"

"Told ya not to worry about him," came her reply.

"But Maw, it's our gold if it was Grandpaws. We could sure use it to ease our living."

About that time the boy heard sounds of a hammer hitting metal. He knew ol' Levi was driving a metal rod down, searching around. He jumped off the porch and ran towards the sound. When he reached the old homeplace, he crouched behind some bushes and watched.

Levi was pounding away on that metal stake. Thud. Thud. Thud. Then came a *clang*, and Levi dropped to his knees. Picking up the dowsing stick, he held it over the stake. It tilted downward, quivering.

Levi jumped to his feet and began dancing around in

the moonlight. He kicked up his heels and clapped his hands. Then he took the shovel and began to dig.

The boy ran home as fast as his legs would carry him. "Maw, Maw!" he called, "Levi's found Grandpaw's gold. He's digging it up this very minute. We've got to stop him!"

His mother was sewing and looked up very unconcerned. "Leave him be."

"But Maw..."

Again she said, "Leave him be!"

So the boy went back and watched as Levi uncovered a heavy iron pot and carried it away, whistling as he went.

The boy returned home feeling cheated and angry as well as sad. When his mother saw him she asked, "Did Levi carry off something?"

"Yes ma'am," the boy said with tears in his eyes. "He carried off a big ol' wash pot full of grandpaw's gold."

"Tweren't gold," she said.

"What do you mean?"

"Tweren't gold in that pot."

"What was it?" he asked.

"Well, your grandpaw buried his favorite huntin' hound in that pot. He covered it up in an oil tarp. All Levi Wiggins is gonna find is a big ol' pot full of bones. Ya' see, son, I took up Grandpaw's gold a long time ago."

They both laughed long and hard, wishing they could have seen Levi's face when he discovered those bones.

This story was shared by oral tradition by a man named Joey Smithson who lives in Hale County. He told it to Bob Watters and he told it to me in the way of true oral tradition. All names were changed to protect the innocent...and the guilty.

The Arduous Journey

Muscle Shoals in Lawrence County, Alabama

The flotilla of flatboats approached the Muscle Shoals on the Tennessee River in 1779. Gunfire rang out as a large band of Cherokee warriors continued their relentless assault on the weary river travelers. It was an assault that had been ongoing for weeks. The sounds of the Tennessee were deafening as the boat's occupants viewed their watery gauntlet. They saw white foam and waves swirling through enormous boulders, piled driftwood and the islands that dotted their path.

The Adventure, largest of the flatboats, was in front. Col. John Donaldson, along with other men on board, was returning gunfire when the swift current grabbed hold of the Adventure. The current swept the careening boat through the shoals. For awhile, no one controlled the boat's rudder.

The women and children were inside the log bunkhouse in the middle of the boat. They huddled together, holding on as best they could. Suddenly young Rachel Donaldson, one of the colonel's daughters, charged out of the bunkhouse and took hold of the rudder handle. The force of the waves ripped it from her grip, almost tossing her into the current. As she fought to hold on, she heard her father calling to her.

"Get back inside the bunkhouse Rachel!"

"No papa," she shouted back, "you need my help."

Some of the warriors running along the river bank pointed to Rachel. She was quite a sight, with her long dark hair billowing in the wind, her skirt flapping around her legs. She held fast to the Adventure's rudder handle though it was much too hard for one person, much less a young girl.

Again her father shouted, "Rachel, get back inside before they kill you." Pointing to two of the men he said, "Take the rudder!"

For a moment Rachel hesitated, then she returned to the safety of the shelter.

Eventually all of the flatboats cleared the shoals. They continued down the Tennessee, and not long after Muscle Shoals the Indians ceased following them. For a while the travelers were able to enjoy the beauty and bounty of what would later become Lawrence County. They camped and rested before continuing their journey. These were the first white settlers to ever see the Tennessee Valley of Alabama.

The Journey to French Lick

The journey began when Colonel John Donaldson and Colonel James Robertson were hired by the Transylvania Company to travel from the edge of Virginia with the purpose of establishing a settlement at French Lick (Nashville, Tennessee) on the Cumberland River. Both Colonel Donaldson and Colonel Robertson were experienced, well educated frontiersman and military leaders as well as able explorers.

Colonel Robertson traveled overland, by way of the Cumberland Gap, following the Warrior's Path part of the way. He was to establish cabins and plant a crop at French Lick ahead of Colonel Donaldson, who made the trip by water in flatboats. Colonel Robertson left first with a company of men, promising if it proved possible he would travel down into the Muscle Shoals area and mark trees near the river so the boat travelers would know if there was a good land crossing from there to French Lick. The passengers would then leave the river and complete their journey overland. (Colonel Robertson never made it as far as Muscle Shoals to mark the trees.)

Colonel Donaldson left Fort Patrick Henry in December 1779. Accompanying Donaldson was his wife and family, as well as Colonel Robertson's wife and family. The families of the men who followed Colonel Robertson were also in this party, as well as a large number of hired men and women with their children. Slaves were also present. Twenty-nine boats started down the Holston River that December. They were to connect with the Tennessee River, then travel up the Ohio to the Cumberland. It would be a journey of 985 miles.

The day the boats left Fort Patrick Henry, it was fiercely cold. The lead boat, the Adventure, belonged to Colonel Donaldson. It was big enough to erect a bunkhouse on deck, complete with a hearth for cooking and warmth.

The flotilla had not traveled far when the Holston River wrapped an icy hand around them, and managed to keep them grounded for almost two months. When the air finally began to warm, the ice melted enough to continue. It was March when they floated past the French Broad River. The days were still cold, but now instead of snow, they faced heavy rains and dense fog. Again the travelers had to halt their journey several times. Strong winds and currents dealt havoc, causing one of the boats to overturn. Not long after passing the French Broad, the party was attacked by Indians. There was no love between the Indians and the settlers at the time, even though in 1730, Sir Alexander Cumming had taken a delegation of seven chiefs to England where a treaty was signed which stated "...love shall flow like a river and peace endure like the mountains." One flatboat was lost when it became snagged. A war party attacked the helpless boat, and all members on board were massacred.

The remainder of the trip to Muscle Shoals was a constant battle with swift currents, narrows, heavy rains, flooding waters, lack of food and general discomfort. The Indian warriors continued to follow the boats, firing on them at every opportunity. Attacks became more frequent as they neared the Shoals.

The Muscle Shoals area was highly valued by the Cherokees. They had been in the Tennessee Valley region long before the invasion by Hernando DeSoto in 1540. The "Singing River" was treasured not only for its beauty, but for its bountiful fish and waterfowl. Wild game was abundant, as were the buffalo. (Buffalo roamed the Shoals area in countless numbers and buffalo paths knee deep reached out in every direction from Lawrence county salt licks until 1826.)

As the flatboats approached the Shoals, the passengers were frightened by the roaring river waters. Their fears were justified as the boats tossed and tumbled their way through the rapids. Once clear of Muscle Shoals they continued to the end of their arduous journey, arriving at French Lick in April, 1770.

By the time they arrived, 23 people had lost their lives by freezing, drowning or killed by hostile attack. This long journey is recorded in American history as one of the hardest journeys ever undertaken by a group of settlers. Young Rachael Donaldson survived the journey. She later married General Andrew Jackson and became a First Lady of the United States of America.

Referances used for this story:

Muscle Shoals History and Folklore - Tennessee Valley Historical Society Vol. 5

The Appalachian Frontier by John A. Caruso, Bobbs-Merrill Co., Inc.

"Get back inside the bunkhouse Rachel!"

"No papa," she shouted back, "you need my help."

Some of the warriors running along the river bank pointed to Rachel. She was quite a sight, with her long dark hair billowing in the wind, her skirt flapping around her legs. She held fast to the Adventure's rudder handle though it was much too hard for one person, much less a young girl.

The Creature

Shelby County, Alabama

Sometimes on warm summer nights when the trees are in full foliage, the mountains in North Shelby county look like huge creatures resting with their rocky ribs exposed by moonlight.

But it is something far more mysterious that is the source of tales Alabamians have long told about an unknown creature. A creature whose cries sound unlike any they've ever heard. A creature whose scream can almost freeze the flow of human blood.

It goes uncaptured—elusive. Yet, there are people in North Shelby who tell of hearing such a creature. Some even claim their forefathers have seen it.

Here is one such tale:
Four boyhood friends left home together one hot July afternoon in 1932. They planned to coon hunt until each caught one. They hunted for table meat, as much as for pleasure.

The leaves on the trees turned upward, a portend of rain. The boys followed two coon hounds tied on ropes. They entered the mountains near Dunnavant and walked a good eight or nine miles before they released the dogs. They planned to hunt back toward home.

As soon as the dogs were free they began running and sniffing the air and ground. They whined and barked as they went, eager to pick up a trail.

The boys followed at first, but it wasn't long until the hounds caught the scent of a coon. Their barks took on a new tone, urgent and excited, and the boys halted. They sat down to listen. They knew every move the hounds were making by their mournful bays. They also knew the moment the coon treed. All four of them jumped to their feet and ran in the direction of the barking sounds. It was a pattern they repeated several times that evening.

The last time the hounds treed, it was pitch dark. The air smelled of rain and the boys heard distant thunder. "We'd better get on home after this one," one boy said. They had three coons at that point.

One of the boys held a lantern as they approached the dogs. Another boy tied the ropes back on the them. The boy with the lantern slowly circled the tree, looking up to catch the eyes of the coon reflected in the light. Suddenly a noise, high pitched and whining, filled the air around them. "What's that?" one asked. The dogs began to whimper.

The boy holding the lantern stared up into the tree's branches and whispered, "There's something up there. It's way up near the top. I can't make it out, but that's no coon!"

Just as he spoke, lightning lit up the area around them. The thunderclap hit—BOOM! It was followed by a blood-curdling scream. The boy dropped the lantern and everything went dark just as the rain started pelting down.

The boys finally managed to light the lantern, and the dogs, wet and shivering, had their tails tucked between their legs. All four boys stood looking up into the tree branches. All four saw the thing, large and dark, its long thick tail hanging down writhing like a serpent. Its eyes reflected clearly in the lantern's light. They were big, round, flashing eyes—watching them. "What is that thing?" they asked in unison. It screamed again, its cry reverberating around them. They raised their guns and started shooting, almost spasmodically. They fired until the shells were used up. Nothing fell. When they looked again, it was gone.

The boys ran through the rain all the way back to Dunnavant. They told their folks what they had seen and heard, but everyone laughed at them. They said the boys really had big imaginations. Yet the boys insisted, "There's a creature out there...there really is a creature out there!"

Thanks to the ladies at the Seventh Heaven Beauty Shop in Columbiana for the idea behind this tale. Thanks especially to Renee Smith, whose mother told her about the unexplained sounds.

Alabama Outsnakes 'Em All

Marshall County, Alabama

The State of Alabama is home to about fifty-nine species of serpents, most of them beneficial to humans in one way or another. Alabamians, like other human beings, have always been both troubled and fascinated by snakes. Some people will tell you these feelings go all the way back to the Garden of Eden when Adam and Eve were mixed up with that wily serpent and got themselves in trouble. Regardless of how it started, wherever folks in Alabama gather to share tales with one another, snakelore is always a popular topic.

Some older beliefs and tales include the one from an old timer who said, "If you drop a horsehair into a bucket of water on a hot summer day, it will turn into a snake."

Another says, "If you're ever out in the woods and get bit by a rattler or copperhead, don't panic. Just look around till you find some snakeweed. Pull it up, chew it, then swallow the juice. That snakeweed will dilute the poison and keep the swelling down."

An old gentleman from DeKalb County once told this tale: "I was working in my garden one day when this big hoop snake comes rollin' down the hill like a big wheel. Well sir, he rolled right into my pear tree, and the poison spike in his tail stuck into that tree. I rushed over and killed that blamed hoop snake, but it was too late. My tree swelled up, split wide open, and died anyhow."

A Jackson County woman tells of hitting a joint snake with her hoe while she was weeding her vegetable patch. "I hit that snake and it shattered into a dozen pieces like an icicle. Then right there before my very eyes I saw those shattered pieces wiggle back together! In no time at all, that snake looked like I had never hit it. It just crawled away. You can't kill a joint snake less' you hit one in the head."

A lady in Cherokee County told about a black racer that chased her one Sunday when she was a little girl. She was on her way home from Sunday School. "At first I ran cause' I'm scared to death of snakes, but then I remembered what my daddy had told me about them racers. So I just stopped and stomped my foot at the thing. That snake turned around and crawled away like I had poured scalding water on it."

Now, there are snake tales and then there are snake tales. *Marshall county seems to hold some kind of title when it comes to big snake tales. Just about anybody in the county will tell you about the giant snake that has been harassing county residents for more than forty years. They say it's a snake you shouldn't mess with and one you will never forget if you ever see it.*

According to all accounts, the Marshall county snake is about as ugly as they come. It is as big as a telephone pole, pale brown with dark black crossbars and a cream-colored belly. This reptile is at least twenty feet long. Evidence indicates that maybe more than one huge snake is living in and around Marshall county. Maybe a whole family of giant hissers, from great-granddaddies to babies, holed up in caves across the county.

Here are some of the more common stories involving the giant snake:

In 1949 a farmer was driving his combine through a Marshall County cornfield when he caught a glimpse of something moving between the corn stalks. He would see it. Then it would vanish. The farmer thought his eyes were playing tricks on him but suddenly an enormous snake lifted its head from the ground right in front of the combine. It slowly rose to a height of ten or eleven feet. The farmer found himself looking up into the reptile's eyes! Those eyes looked like huge slits. The snake's tongue darted in and out.

The farmer didn't sit still very long. He threw his combine into reverse and ripped a path through the cornfield in his haste to get away from that snake. He lost most of his corn crop that summer because he refused to return to his fields.

A fellow from around Albertsville saw the snake sometime in 1957. He told of riding his mule to go rabbit hunting one day. When he got tired, he decided to get off and rest. He tied his mule to a tree and lay down on the ground with his head against a log, putting the rabbits he had shot down beside him. He hadn't rested long when that log started moving! It wasn't a log at all. It was a snake. The snake ended up eating all his rabbits. And then his mule.

About 1961 two men and a small boy went fishing on Guntersville Lake. They rowed into a small cove where large rock boulders covered the mountainside. The fishermen were busy getting their lines and hooks into the water and didn't notice an enormous snake crawling out of a cave opening just a little distance up the mountain. By the time the snake's head reached the water's edge, the boy saw it. "Gosh," he yelled. "Look at that *big* ol' snake!"

Both men were laughing and joking with one another, but when they heard the boy yell, they glanced in the direction he was pointing and saw the monstrous ophidian! They began to holler, and, beat the sides of their boat with paddles. Undaunted, the snake glided into the water, swimming straight for their boat. It rammed them! The boat flipped over, dumping all three fisherman into the water. They started swimming for shore just as fast as they could.

Once safely on the shore, they watched as the snake swam down the cove and out across the main lake. Later one of the men said, "Hardest thing I ever did was swim back out to my boat. You just can't begin to imagine how big that snake was!"

The most recent sighting of the giant snake was near Warrenton. Three high school boys went fishing on a hot July day in 1992. They were catfish fishing with some terrible smelling liver. (Catfish think rotted liver smells like sirloin steak.) It was a good day for catin', and it wasn't long until the boys had about twelve nice size fish on their stringer. They were talking and watching their floats when they heard a loud hissing/whirling sound behind them. When they turned around, they saw this gigantic pale brown snake not more than five yards away from them! The snake's head appeared to be about twelve inches across. The snake was raised off the ground a good six feet, swaying side to side like a cobra. The boys jumped to their feet, but every time one of them tried to run, the serpent leaned in that direction. "Stand still," the first boy shouted. "Let's just stand still and see what it wants."

"What if it wants us?" The second boy cried.

"Look at it," the third boy shouted. "It's a monster!"

Then the first boy spoke again, "Let's pull up the catfish and toss them to it."

The third boy was too scared to move, but the second one yanked the catfish out of the water, twirling the stringer around his head. When he let go of the stringer, it sailed through the air. The snake caught those fish in mid-air. Then it crawled away with that stringer dangling out of either side of its mouth. When the snake was gone, all three boys collapsed onto the ground.

Sources: Newspaper articles from The Birmingham News *and* Sand Mountain Lookout, *Jim Pate, Southern*

History Department-Birmingham Public Library; Jasper Brown, Primary Councelor-Fellowship House, Birmingham; Crossville elementary and high school teachers; Robert O. Johnson, Guntersville.

It Happened on the Back Forty

Cleburne County, Alabama

Moonshine is as much a part of the fabric of Alabama history as dirt roads, watermelon patches, cold water wells, or fried chicken. Most of the state had active stills at one time or another. On the surface this tale is about the moonshine business, but its also the tale of two brothers, a stranger, and many vipers. They all become entangled with one another as the result of an unusual competition.

The story begins around 1917. At that time there were certain residents living in Cleburne County who depended on moonshine production for all or part of their income. Many were displaced farmers who had found a new vocation. Cleburne County wasn't alone in this manufacturing effort. Many Alabamians were involved in like ventures. What made Cleburne County notable were the Franklin Brothers, Creed and Alvin Franklin. Some say they produced the finest home brew in the whole state. Maybe the whole country.

The Franklin's came from a long line of processors. A line that stretched back across the generations through their Scotch-Irish ancestry all the way to Europe. The recipe for "fixin's" was an heirloom that had been proudly and carefully preserved. The family business evolved as fathers taught sons, one generation after another.

In l917 the family consisted of Grandma Franklin, her six grown children, and their respective families. They all lived within walking distance of one another—all except two of the adult children, and they had moved away.

The Franklin's were farmers, as well as moonshiners. They raised both produce (especially corn), and cattle on their 400 acres. Grandma kept a large vegetable garden, and a flock of chickens.

Creed Franklin was the eldest son. He was a man of medium build, blue eyes, and sandy-colored hair. He had a good sense of humor, and a quick mind. Creed was the primary family business manager.

Alvin Franklin was three years younger than his brother. While he favored Creed as far as hair and eye color, he was a large, powerfully built man who possessed a hair-trigger temper. Many people thought Alvin couldn't talk. This was because he rarely spoke a word out loud to anyone except close family members unless he was angry.

The business, "White Mule" as some old timers called it, distilled a clear, transparent, potent drink of fine quality. It was old-fashioned corn whiskey made in solid copper stills. Each of the six stills had pots that produced upward of 500 gallons. Fermentation took 13 to 16 days, then the finished product was bottled and aged. Business was good. Customers ranged west to Birmingham, east to Atlanta, as far south as Mobile and New Orleans, and north to Nashville. The Franklins considered it a matter of pride that folks in Tennessee liked to buy from them. Most of the business, however, was local or in-state.

In November of that year, a stranger moved into Cleburne County. He bought a farm about twelve miles from the Franklin Brothers, and he started a "business" that quickly rivaled theirs. This fellow had moved from Harlan County, Kentucky and possessed an heirloom recipe all his own.

It didn't take Creed or Alvin very long to realize just how fickle the paying public could be. The long steady line coming to their doorsteps began to ebb and flow like an ocean tide. Folks just couldn't make up their minds whom to buy from.

One day Alvin asked, "What we gonna' do, Creed?"

With a troubled expression on his face Creed answered, "I don't rightly know, Alvin. I'm spending a lot of time thinking about it though."

"Why don't we just shoot the son-of-a-gun." Alvin's face was flushed with anger. "Danged intruder, why'd he come here anyhow?"

Creed shook his head. "Can't shoot him Alvin, cause' it would bring the law down on us. 'Sides, we can beat this feller. We just got to come up with a good idea. I think maybe it's time for you and me to pay him a little visit."

"I'll get my gun."

"No, Alvin. I told ya, no shooting."

The Franklin Brothers paid the Kentuckian a visit that week. They talked with him about their mutual interests and eventually discussed business.

"Now the way I see it," said Creed, "we're gonna all end up losing if we can't come up with a workable plan that guarantees us a profit. I've got an idea that may work real good. It'll be fair to all of us. I was thinkin' we can hold a contest on my back forty acres. It backs up against thick, hilly woods. The oaks grow big back there and give plenty of shade. We can start an annual 4th of July get together. We'll serve all the Bar-B-Q folks can eat, and involve the church ladies by letting them sell handmades and baked goods."

The stranger was smiling and nodding his head, but Alvin just sat quietly, looking at the floor.

Creed continued, "Invitation will be by word-of-mouth, and I believe we'll have a good turn out. We'll put up some tables off away from the Bar-B-Q, back next to the woods. We'll put wash tubs on the tables and I'll fill two with my brew, you can fill two with yours. Then we'll let those who want to, ease on back there and sample all they please. The samplers can vote on which batch of moonshine is the best.

The winner takes all the local business for a period of one year. What you do out of the county is up to you."

"Sounds good to me," said the stranger. He and Creed shook hands, but Alvin just nodded his head.

The first 4th of July was a smashing success. Word-of-mouth traveled just fine and about two hundred people came down the dirt road that led to the far back pasture. Men, women and children showed up. Mother's even brought their babies along. It was a time before moonshine had earned a bad name.

All the Franklin women were active in the church, so the ladies brought lots of pies and cakes, potato salad and baked beans, cabbage slaw and deviled eggs. They also brought several types of home made breads to eat and sell along with craft items such as quilts, aprons, bonnets and such.

The Franklin's had two pony carts set up for the children to ride in, along with plenty of fireworks for later in the evening. Of course, the samplers didn't need the fireworks because they got theirs out of the galvanized tubs!

The Franklin Brothers won the contest that first 4th of July, and the Kentuckian won it the second year. The third year, the Franklin's won again but almost lost because they kept finding diamond-back rattlesnakes in their wash tubs. Alvin got mad and almost started a fight because he accused the Kentuckian of sneaking the snakes into the tubs. Creed finally convinced him it wasn't true. They found three snakes that year.

By the fourth year it seemed they were pulling snakes out of the tubs every hour or so. Two diamond-backs were found in the Kentuckian's tubs, and three diamond-backs along with one copperhead were found in the Franklin tubs. It got so bad they almost canceled the contest, but the samplers bravely fished the pacified snakes out and killed 'em.

When the fifth year of the annual celebration rolled around they had to call the whole thing off. Why that back pasture was literally crawling with hundreds of venomous snakes—rattlesnakes and copperheads. There were even some water moccasins crawling around. It wasn't a fit place for man nor beast!

The stranger left Alabama in the Fall of 1921. He sold his farm and returned to Kentucky. Alvin got into a fight that year and got himself shot. Both he and grandma died within months of each other. Creed didn't have much heart for the business after that. The Franklin stills were never found or busted, but Creed cut way back on production until eventually he stopped producing altogether. Moonshine was frowned upon more and more, and the "revenooers" were getting better at finding stills. Creed didn't want himself or any of his family to end up in jail and that's why he found a legal business the family could buy. The business continues to this very day.

The pasture where the old contest used to take place is really beautiful, but it remains snake infested. Old habits are hard to break once they're formed. Very few people in Cleburne county can even recall those 4th of July contests anymore.

An elderly, retired moonshiner shared this tale with me. He prefers to remain anonymous for obvious reasons. Real names and locations have been changed. It is a fact that Jefferson, Cleburne, Marshall and Colbert counties, in that order, once held the dubious title of being the state's largest moonshine manufacturers.

Beware of the milk-white stone...it means trouble. This one sits alongside a road in Maylene, Alabama.

The Milk-White Stone

Shelby County, Alabama

An old couple owned several hundred acres of farmland near Calera in the Spring of 1917. Their house sat back off the road behind a stand of piney woods. Their cleared fields stretched out just beyond the backyard.

The kitchen window offered a good view of the fields. One morning, while the missus was washing her breakfast dishes, she noticed something standing about midway out in one field. The morning was foggy, so at first she didn't pay much attention. Whatever it was, it was white, so there was no mistaking it was there. Finally, the missus put on her coat and went out the back door. She crossed the yard and, standing at the field's edge, she hollered, "Who are you?"

The thing never moved nor answered. She put her hand up over her eyes, straining to see it better. Then she started out across the field. When she was about ten feet from it, she stopped..

It looked like some sort of milk-white alabaster stone. It wasn't as tall as she was, and not nearly so round. She walked up and touched it. The stone felt smooth and cool beneath her fingers. *Where'd you come from?* she puzzled.

When her husband walked into the house that evening, she took his hand and led him out into the field so he could see the milk-white stone. He scratched his head. "Weirdest thing I ever saw," he said. "It wasn't here when I plowed yesterday." He put his arms around the rock and managed to lift it, with effort.

"I'll bring my wagon out tomorrow," he told her. "I'll carry it off somewhere out in the woods."

"Don't do that," she said. "It's so pretty...I never seen a rock so pretty. Let's put it in my flower garden next to the house."

So the farmer got his wagon and moved the milk-white stone to the flower garden next to the house. It looked beautiful there.

The farmer and his wife weren't rich people, but their house was warm. They had plenty to eat, and joy was present so they lived a good life. However, just two days after they moved the milk-white stone to the flower garden, their fresh water well went dry. They primed and primed, but the water wouldn't come. The farmer had to hitch the mule to his wagon every few days and travel some distance to the spring-fed creek to fetch fresh water. It was a bother.

A week later, their milk cow ran off. The farmer hunted and hunted, but he never found her. He had to hitch his mule to the wagon, go down to his neighbor's farm, and buy another cow. It was expensive.

When the barn caught fire two weeks later, they managed to save the goats and other livestock. Their friends eventually held a barn raising for them and that was good, but it was a terrible hardship just the same.

When the hornet's nest blew out of the giant tulip poplar right on top of the old man's head while he was cutting firewood, they both began to wonder. The pain put him to bed for days.

One morning during breakfast, the missus says, "I been thinking. We've had us a string of bad luck. It never started until we found that milk-white stone. I think you best carry it off some place else —far away from here."

The farmer knew that she was right, so the very next day he hitched his mule to his wagon and loaded the stone into the back. He drove about ten miles down the road and deposited the stone on the sandy bank of a shallow creek. Sure enough, the bad luck ended. In fact, the runaway milk cow came back so now they had two. The next spring their livestock produced better than they ever had. The well even started to flow again.

Somewhere on the sandy bank of a shallow creek, another farmer found a beautiful milk-white stone and took it home with him to use as a step for his front door.

The miseries he suffered are too numerous to detail.

It's been going on like that for a long time now. Why that stone's been moved more times than a dog has fleas. Some folks bring it home for its stark white beauty. For others, it seems to just show up on its own.

If you chance to find a stone that fits this description on your property, don't you take any chances. Go on and carry it off some place else. The stone means trouble—a bothersome, expensive, hardship kind of trouble.

The idea behind this folktale is very old. Its roots are in Europe, and it came to Alabama with early settlers. Folklorist Margaret Gillis Figh mentions it in the Alabama Review, Vol. 16. Mrs. Faye Baxley, Calera, Alabama, gave a wonderful description of a "white thing" appearing in a field to her grandmother a long time ago.

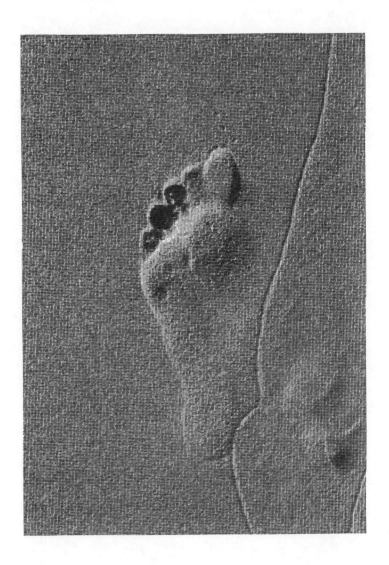

Tecumseh's Footprint

Tallapoosa County, Alabama

The warriors came, in the early morning dawn, riding their ponies alongside their Chief, the mighty Tecumseh. Their journey from the high mountains had been long, and now they began the homeward trek. The year was 1811. Tecumseh had come to Tukabatchee joined in alliance with the great King of the English who lived across the seas. He rode with war on his lips and flames in his eyes.

The warriors glided through the woodlands like spirit-owls, strong and silent. They moved through the heavy fog-laden morning air, following the banks of the Tallapoosa to Kialijee where Tecumseh's kinsman dwelled. His kinsman welcomed them, and fed them a breakfast of fish, corn mush, and berries.

Tecumseh's heart was heavy, but his passion was fresh. He had gone to Tukabatchee to join the nations of the Creek in a united war. He had expected a positive reply, but it did not come as he had foreseen. The Creeks were of divided opinion. Now as he sat with his mother's people, "words of fire" spilled from his mouth.

"Come!" he shouted. "Join me in this great war cry against the Americans. Together we will unite the tribes and nations. These unrestrained settlers who have usurped and encroached upon our lands with wagons rolling ever forward while they scatter like the leaves blown on the wind. They break our treaties as a storm breaks the branches of a tree. No more! Together we can free our lands once and for all. We will take back that which is ours by rightful birth! Will you take the War Path my family? Will you be part of my war cry?"

They listened, Tecumseh's kinsman, as some of them had listened at Tukabatchee. They saw the flame in his eyes. Their hearts were deeply stirred by his words. Yet, they hesitated. How could they carry the red-painted war club to all the tribes and nations? It was a thing for prophets and chiefs to decide. They were just ordinary people. How could they fight against the seemingly endless hordes of soldiers and wagons? Peace was what they wanted. "No," they answered. "Let us walk the path of peace. We wish only to live our lives in peace."

Enraged Tecumseh cried, "Cowards! How can you be my kinsman? Dogs have more courage than you! Woe be to you and your children. Do you think these enemies will allow you peace? No! They will surely drive you from the land of your ancestors. Never again will you dwell or hunt in these green forests. Never again will you fish in these cool streams. They will not rest until you are driven away—or killed. You will become less than dogs!"

Then, Great Tecumseh stamped his foot, and lo, the earth shook! Long after he and his warrior's returned to Kentucky, Tecumseh's footprint remained embedded in solid rock! It remains embedded even to this modern day, almost 200 years later.

Somewhere on Kialijee creek, on Lake Martin in Tallapoosa county, you will find a small island. On this island there rests a large boulder undaunted by wind, rain, snow or time. Embedded in the boulder remains the outline of Great Tecumseh's footprint.

Taken from an ancient legend. General Sam Dale wrote that Tecumseh returned to Tippicanoe before he stamped his foot, but we like this legend best.

"Cowards! How can you be my kinsman? Dogs have more courage than you! Woe be to you and your children. Do you think these enemies will allow you peace? No! They will surely drive you from the land of your ancestors. Never again will you dwell or hunt in these green forests. Never again will you fish in these cool streams. They will not rest until you are driven away—or killed. You will become less than dogs!"

—Chief Tecumseh

Ordeal on the Tombigbee

Baldwin and Mobile Counties

Land and River Pirates

On the open sea, even today, robbers and looters are sometimes referred to as pirates. In the 1700s and early 1800s many treacherous pirates sailed The Spanish Main capturing ships traveling to and from Europe and America. These pirates robbed any boat that was weaker than their own. Pirate ships were usually armed with powerful cannons.

Until the early 1800s certain rivers, trails (especially the Natchez Trace) and, later, roads were infested with land and river pirates. Some of the famous land pirates were Micajah and Wiley Harp, two erratic brothers who became known as the "Two Mad Harpes." There was also Joseph Thompson Hare, Samuel Mason, and John A. Murrell. Later the Copeland Gang was active. Both the river pirates and the land pirates were the bitter fruit of the pioneers who settled the frontier. It seemed the wilderness had a strange effect on anyone who spent much time in it. Some referred to it as "blood madness." Like the pioneers, these outlaws could be savage, and were often filled with a *fierce implacable energy. The wilderness hid them, inspired them, and concealed them. River pirates plied their trade on the inland rivers. They were heavily armed.*

During the period before 1798, Alabama was dominated by international rivalry. The French and English had a tug of war for Alabama lands and the Spanish kept a strong foothold, especially right after the American Revolution. In 1785, Georgia pushed claims for Alabama lands and a dispute with Spain followed. By 1798, the Mississippi Territory was formed. European and Canadian trappers were active, but there were few settlers until around 1810. What few settlers there were, were often isolated. Land and river pirates took advantage of the fact that settlements were scattered.

At first there were no real roads to speak of, so travel by land usually followed game and hunting paths or Indian trading trails. (The Wolf Trail and the Great Trading Path were two.) The main trading routes were rivers. Steamboats did not come into use until after 1818, so flatboats, keelboats, barges, canoes and a cypress dugout called a pirogue were used on Alabama waterways. Travel down river wasn't so much a hardship as trying to get back upriver. Travel in either direction could take many long, slow, arduous months to accomplish a round trip. Flatboats were often ripped apart at journey's end and the return trip was by canoe or land travel. Regardless of the trip's direction, boat power was furnished by hand: rowing, poling, and sometimes pulling the boat from the shoreline. Sails were used with keelboats when the wind prevailed.

River travelers were open to Indian attacks, yet the greatest danger did not come from these native people, but rather from robbers. Great numbers of them built rough living quarters, or lived in caves along the riverbanks. They preyed on travelers along all of Alabama's navigable rivers. The larger the population grew, the greater the number of pirates. Many kept boats hidden in the mouths of streams to quickly descend on hapless victims as they moved on the rivers. Creeks were often dreaded by river travelers.

The Ordeal

There was once a river pirate by the name of Jean Claude d'Artaguette. This was not his true name, only one he used. He frequented the Alabama and Mississippi coastal lands, traveling up the inland rivers. In 1737, a band of Canadian fur trappers set out on the Tombigbee River bound for Mobile. These were rough, hard-fighting men. Most of the time they did their trading in Mobile; however when prices were too low, they would travel on to New Orleans to trade. After the trading was finished and they had rested a while, they returned upriver with necessary supplies of salt, coffee, sugar, etc. Either way, the river pirates saw the shipments as good fortune.

On that fateful day in 1737, the fur traders had paddled their five pirogues down river filled with all types of hides: wolf, fox, beaver, deer, otter, muskrat and more. It was their habit to camp along the bank in the evenings, when all seemed quite, and there was no threat of attack.

This was a day when Jean Claude d'Artaguette and his band waited in the backwaters, near where the Tensaw flows close to the Tombigbee after it has joined the Mobile River. There the land spreads out into bayous and swamps and forests. It was a perfect place to hide river rats. They had seen the trappers and quietly followed them downriver. Then they hid in the woods.

When the traders had their camp set up, the pirates descended on them with the swiftness of hunting hawks. They soon took possession of the camp, encountering little resistance. Two black slaves were with the fur traders. Their names were Johnny Man and Bosard. Both slaves responded to their capture, not with fear, but with much joy—dancing and laughing. "Good!" they shouted. "We can't be any worse off. How we hate these filthy fur traders. Let us join you. Make pirates of us. We will cook. We will fight. We will be loyal to you."

For some reason d'Artaguette liked the slaves and accepted them into his band. "We will barter with these

Frenchman," he said. "I know chiefs who will pay well for the pleasure of slitting their throats!" Much laughter followed his comment. Johnny Man and Bosard clapped their hands and sang for the entertainment of the pirates. They remained at the campsite another full day. Disarmed, the fur traders were allowed a measure of freedom, for the pirates outnumbered them two to one.

The next morning Johnny Man brought the traders their breakfast. As he gave them their food, he whispered a plan to them for overcoming the pirates and regaining their boats. When the traders realized that Johnny Man and Bosard had been pretending all along, they agreed to do as Johnny Man instructed.

Johnny Man and Bosard caught many fish and cooked a wonderful gumbo type soup. That evening when they served the pirates their dinner, Johnny Man stood behind d'Artaguette holding the large pot of hot gumbo. He suddenly dumped it on top of d'Artaguette's head. The pirate screamed in pain! Johnny Man then hit him with the empty pot. This stunned the pirate even more. Johnny Man picked d'Artaguette up, bodily tossing him into the river. The pirate's gun was dislodged and Johnny Man picked it up. The moment that Johnny Man dumped the gumbo on d'Artgaguette's head, Bosard immediately started a fight, and the fur traders joined him slamming their fists against the pirates jaws. A vicious melee followed. Guns were fired, and when it ended more than half of the pirates were dead. The others managed to escape. When the ordeal ended, the traders sank the pirate's boats. They left for Mobile that very night.

Both Johnny Man and Bosard were given their freedom for saving the traders and their cargo. Bosard stayed in the Mobile area, but Johnny Man continued to work as a cook for the traders. He later became an independent fur trader himself.

Some of this story was gleaned from oral tradition in Mobile.

The Rival

Walker County, Alabama

H.F. DeBardelaben owned a farm near Sipsey. He raised cattle. Just after World War II, H.F. was eager to find a heat-tolerant strain that would thrive during Alabama's hottest, driest months. This was the reason he bought a 2,400-pound bull and kept it in a pasture across the Sipsey Branch of the Warrior River, away from the main farm and away from "the ladies." It was a fine, powerful bull.

H.F. was a well-to-do, intelligent man. He had the know how to keep his finances on better-than-average footing, but he wasn't a miser. Not only did he love cattle, but he also loved beautiful things, like cars.

It was hard to buy a car after the war. You had to get your name on a waiting list. When Cadillac came out with its big, sleek Fleetwood model, H.F. wanted one. He put his name on the list and waited his turn. He had to wait more than two years. When the Cadillac finally arrived, it was red—Alabama Red. H.F. petted that car like a favorite child. When he wasn't working, he took long rides in it.

There was a little cottage over in the bull's pasture, and one day H.F. drove over in his army jeep. He had some work to do in the cottage. He hadn't been gone long when his foreman received a phone call saying, "We need H.F. for some important business in Birmingham. This is urgent."

There wasn't a phone in the cottage and it was too far to walk. All the farm vehicles were in use, so when the foreman saw the keys in the Fleetwood, he jumped at the opportunity to drive that gorgeous hunk of Detroit artistry! Revving up the engine, the foreman glided through town, across the river to the pasture.

Three gates led into it. The foreman stopped each time to open and close the gates, but he left the third one open, believing that he and H.F. would be coming right back. When he arrived, he found H.F. hard at work and determined to finish the task. The foreman, pushing up his sleeves, joined in the work.

Meanwhile the bull came over a small hill and noticed something glittering in the sunlight. Curious, he trotted toward it and because the gate was open, he was soon standing three feet from the driver's side of the new auto. It wasn't the car's color that caused a bad reaction in the bull. What he saw standing there in front of him was another 2,400 pound bull. Bulls cannot tolerate rivals. At first he stood there tossing his head. Then, as his eyes narrowed and his nostrils flared, he snorted fire, and pawed the ground three times. Lowering his head, he rammed the car. SMASH! Backing off he still saw his competitor, so again he lowered his head and pawed the ground three times. Bellowing loudly, he rammed the car a second time. When he looked, the other bull was still standing there, wounded but unfazed. By now, H.F.'s bull had white foam all around his mouth from the excitement. He stood there tossing his head as if to clear it, then he lowered it and rammed the car a third time. BOOM! When he backed off the offending bull had disappeared.

A pond lay on the other side of the Fleetwood. The bull was sweating and thirsty, so he trotted around the car to enjoy a refreshing drink. All was well until he turned around. When he did, he froze! There stood his antagonist, reflected on the passenger's side of the Caddie, starring at him as though nothing had happened.

Rage coursed through the bull's veins. He lowered his

head and charged with the strength of a locomotive. His horns remained imbedded for a few minutes until he finally managed to free them by slowly twisting his head from side to side. He backed off, once his head was free. The rival was still there. The bull gave a furious shake of his head, pawed the ground, and charged his enemy two more times. When he finished, the other bull was truly gone! He trotted around the car looking slowly to the left, then to the right, and when he reached the trunk area, he kicked hard with both hind legs. He managed to cave in the entire trunk. Then the bull walked peacefully through the gate and out of sight.

All this time H.F. and his foreman were watching the skirmish, but they could only stand in the doorway of the cottage and shout abusive words at the bull. It was all they could do.

The bull was never troubled by any other challengers, and lived happily ever after.

This story was told by the Reverend John L. Ebaugh III of Birmingham, Alabama.

Wake up, Amos!

Morgan County, Alabama

They have a saying over in Decatur. Some folks say it has been around just about as long as anyone can remember, and will most likely continue to be used as long as Decatur stands. There is a story behind this saying that goes something like this:

The farmlands around Decatur are beautiful, lush, green fields that stretch out across the horizon. Like so many cities in Alabama, Decatur is growing. Signs of suburbia are everywhere. One by one, vast expanses of green are giving way to subdivisions. Folks who live in these newly abandoned crop fields have met with the determination of the local field mice. Some new homes have been virtually overrun with the tiny vermin. Frantic calls are made to exterminators.

Eighty-five years ago, Decatur's growth was on a much smaller scale, yet in 1912, there were homes on the edge of town, and residents fought battles with persistent field mice. Only back then the exterminators were the four-legged variety—the ever vigilant cats!

Amos McCorkel lived in a tumble-down house on the northern edge of Decatur. He lived there with his wife, Rosealee, and their 16 stairstep children. Amos was a jack of all trades, seeking work wherever and whenever he could find it. He was nearing middle age, had an angular face, thick black hair and a slender physique.

The McCorkle children resembled field mice in many ways. They were small of stature, the oldest boy not an inch over five-feet-four. All the children had big brown eyes, sandy hair, and cauliflower ears.

Mrs. McCorkle, bless her heart, was a short, plain woman. She could never be accused of being a "do-all" woman. To the contrary, she ran her household on an ecological balance that was based upon jungle law, "eat or be eaten." Thus insects, like ants, roaches and silverfish—even spiders—had no effect on her. She paid no attention whatsoever to the field mice. In fact, none of the McCorkles seemed to notice or care that their homeplace resembled a junkyard.

The house was sparsely furnished. A table and two chairs sat in the kitchen, along with two old boards propped up on bricks. These were used as a type of deacon's bench for the children. Two worn chairs with the stuffing hanging out sat in the parlor, along with a pitiful table that held a kerosene lamp. The floor was bare, worn wood. Each of the two bedrooms contained a wooden bed with roping tied across the frame to hold the chicken feather mattresses. There were other thin, pallet-like feather mattresses scattered around on the floors of each bedroom. Pillows and rags were stuffed into broken windows, and newsprint, along with old clothing, covered the walls. This served as a type of insulation.

The roof sagged badly. The timbers were rotting because the roof leaked like a sieve when it rained. Multiple buckets and jars plunked out wild rhythms while catching the rain that fell indoors. During such moments, Rosealee would shout, "You got to fix the roof Amos!"

"I will," he would call back to her, "soon as the rain stops." Then later, when it was dry, no one seemed to give it another thought.

If the inside of the house looked bad, it was a palace compared to the outside. A rusted old fence encircled the yard. Everything the McCorkles ever owned but no longer desired lay in the yard, both front and back. There were old buckets, washtubs, wagon wheels, broken crockery, clothing and shoes. A variety of ropes and wire lay on the ground, along side of small animal bones, skulls, chicken feathers, old fruit jars and watermelon rinds. Food scraps were piled on one side of the back yard. Some people might have called this putrefied mass of victuals a compost pile, but if it was, the McCorkles were not aware of it. It not only looked awful, it smelled awful. Yet, it provided a type of *Mouse Heaven* for the field mice. The McCorkel's kept a large assortment of breeding cats, but the mice far outnumbered them.

Major Thomas Blackwell lived down the road from the McCorkles. He was their opposite in every way. The major was military to the core. He was disciplined, organized, commanding, methodical, tidy and very business minded. He owned a beautiful white frame, two-story house with a wide wrap-around front porch. He had a large barn, several outbuildings, an assortment of livestock and several hundred acres of neat, well-tended crop fields.

Major Blackwell was a man of few vices, save perhaps a bit too much fondness for fine whiskey. It stood to reason that Amos McCorkle and his family represented sheer chaos to the Major—something he despised, but was forced to tolerate.

He could see their hovel quite clearly from his upstairs bedroom window. He also had to walk past their property every time he followed the path into Decatur. It was frustrating.

One evening Amos McCorkle arrived home feeling very tired. He went to bed not long after dinner. He had parked his tool cart beside the front gate, intending to move it later, but forgot and left it there. It was the same evening the major went into Decatur for an early dinner and camaraderie with some of his friends.

Upon returning home that evening, the major was having a problem focusing. He mistook a horse, tied to a gate post, to be a young woman. Removing his cap, he said to her, "Good evening young lady. Don't you think you should be getting on towards home?" The horse switched its tail across his face.

"Good heaven's woman, I'm not trying to be fresh. I just thought I might escort you home safely." Again, the horse swatted him.

"All right, stay. I certainly won't bother you any more." With that, the Major continued his journey. The moon kept hiding behind the clouds, causing him to stray off the path. By the time he reached the McCorkel's house, everyone in that family was fast asleep. Everyone, that is, except the mice and cats, who were playing hide and seek both inside and outside the house.

Major Blackwell failed to see the tool cart parked beside the front gate. He stumbled over it, hitting the ground with a *thud*. Climbing back onto his feet, the major held a pick ax in his right hand. He bawled, "Blast you Amos McCorkle," and twirling the pick ax around his head a few times, he let go of it. The major watched as the ax hurled toward the house.

It flew across the yard and crashed through a bedroom window, shattering glass everywhere. The ax continued to sail across the bed where Amos and Rosealee were sleeping. Then it smashed into the wall. The impact separated the pick from the ax handle. Both bounced down onto the floor where four McCorkle children were sleeping. The pick hit a large crockery jar, shattering it. The handle bounced back up and hit a cat. It leaped into the air, claws extended, catching Rosealee by her arm as she jumped out of the bed. By now, the cat was yowling, the children were crying, Rosalee was screaming, and confusion reigned. Amos, however, slept like a newborn.

"Wake up Amos, my God! The cat's broke ever dish in the house!" Rosealee yelled as she picked up the ax handle and walloped him with it. Poor Amos came up off the bed like a Boston bare knuckle fighter.

All this time Major Blackwell stood motionless, out

beside the front gate, listening to the uproar. It was sobering! In the quite night air every sound carried as though it was being played over a loud speaker. The Major tarried long enough to be sure no one was hurt, then quietly slipped on home.

A few nights later, the Major shared the story with some of his friends in Decatur. They all had a good laugh. The story has been repeated ever since and the saying has lived. Every time a catastrophic noise or happening occurs around Decatur people say, "Wake up Amos, my God! The cat's broke ever dish in the house!"

We must tell you that the McCorkle roof finally collapsed, and the family moved to another dwelling. Major Blackwell bought their land, leveling the house and clearing away all the debris. He installed a fence around all his property, with a big gate, and a sign that read: "KEEP OUT, ESPECIALLY McCORKLES!" The major was quite happy after that, though he did continue to have a problem with field mice.

This story was taken from the Decatur Family Weekly, *1974, and has been adapted.*

About the Author

Sarah Jane Turnbow Tackett was born in Russelville, Arkansas. Her childhood years were spent in Little Rock and Texarkana. Sarah had a lively childhood, learning to ride all types of livestock and mixing with real cowboys at the North Little Rock Horse and Mule Auction Barns where her grandfather worked. It was around these livestock barns that she learned chewing tobacco didn't taste like a homemade brownie!

Sarah has lived in Alabama for a total of 32 years and considers herself an Alabamian. Both she and her husband John have deep family roots in Alabama. (Both family histories pre-date the Civil War. Sarah's in Perry County, and John's in Talladaga and other counties.)

Sarah is a teller of tales both large and small. She is a listener as well as a storyteller and writer. Sarah has been an active oral storyteller for almost 30 years. A member of the National Story League, and past member of the Southern Order of Storytellers, Sarah co-founded the Birmingham Tale-Spinners Story League in 1971. The group is composed of volunteer storytellers.

Sarah Jane edited and updated the National Story League's Handbook for Junior Storytellers which has sold across the United States. *Story Art Magazine*, a magazine for oral storytellers has published many of Sarah's poems and stories. *Story Art* is a publication of the National Story League.

She spent eight years, working as an artist within school systems across the state sponsored by the Alabama State Council on the Arts, Artist In Education Program. Sarah worked in both short and long term residencies in elementary schools, middle schools and high schools. She used oral storytelling as a folk art, teaching students and teachers the value of the oral tale and creative writing.

Sarah was a featured teller in The Atlanta Storytelling Festival and Old Christmas Story Festival in Atlanta, Georgia; The Detroit Storytelling Festival, Detroit, Michigan; The Alabama State Storytelling Festival, Selma; Storytelling Festival of Dothan; Marshall County Storytelling Festival, Guntersville; City Fest and the Children's Hands-On Museum in Tuscaloosa; Storytelling Festival in Lafayette; Polk-Salat Festival, Arab; Storytelling in Mobile and Fairhope; Fort Deposit Arts Festival, Ft. Deposit; A Program of Storytelling for Chicago Suburban Libraries, Chicago, Illinois.Sarah Jane is a member of the Birmingham Quill Club, and the Alabama Writer's Conclave.

She has been happily married to John H. Tackett for 40 years. They live on a small farm in Chelsea with their two dogs: Jackson and Hobo; and one cat: Muffin. John retired in 1997 as an aquatic biologist in water pollution studies with Southern Company Services. He spent six months in 1997 hiking the Appalachian Trail from Georgia to Maine. The Tackett's are members of Christ Charismatic Episcopal Church in Fairfield.

They have two grown daughters, Caroline and Rebecca. Caroline teaches fourth grade at Southminster Presbyterian Church, and Rebecca is an Alcohol and Drug Counselor with the Fellowship House in Birmingham.

This is Sarah Jane's first book.